SOLVING
INFORMATION ASSURANCE ISSUES
USING
DEFENSE IN DEPTH MEASURES
AND THE
ANALYTICAL HIERARCHY PROCESS

RODNEY ALEXANDER

Abstract

Organizational computing devices are increasingly becoming targets of cyber-attacks, and organizations have become dependent on the safety and security of their computer networks and their organizational computing devices. Business and government often use defense in-depth information assurance measures such as firewalls, intrusion detection systems, and password procedures across their enterprises to plan strategically and manage IT security risks. This quantitative study explores whether the analytical hierarchy process (AHP) model can be effectively applied to the prioritization of information assurance defense in-depth measures. In response to these threats, the President, legislators, experts, and others have characterized cybersecurity as a pressing national security issue. The methods used in this study consisted of emailing study participants a survey requesting that they prioritize five defense in-depth information assurance measures, anti-virus, intrusion detection, password, smart-cards, and encryption, with a range of responses from 1-5 using a Likert scale to consider standard cost, effectiveness, and perceived ease of use in terms of protection of organizational computing devices. The measures were then weighted, based on ranking. A pair-wise comparison of each of the five measures were then made using AHP to determine whether the Likert scale and the AHP model could be effectively applied to the prioritization of information assurance measures to protect organizational computing devices. The findings of the research reject the H_0 null hypothesis that AHP does not affect the relationship between the information technology analysts' prioritization of five defense in-depth dependent variables and the independent variables of cost, ease of use, and effectiveness in protecting organizational devices against cyber-attacks.

Dedication

I dedicate this manuscript to my mentor, Dr. John Grillo.

Acknowledgments

I would like to acknowledge U.S. information technology analysts who are critical to the protection of information computing devices in the United States.

Table of Contents

List of Tables

List of Figures

CHAPTER 1. INTRODUCTION

Organizations have become dependent on the safety and security of their computer networks and their organizational computing devices. However, organizational computing devices such as desktops, notebooks, and smart phones are increasingly becoming targets of cyber-attacks. Information technology (IT) has evolved into its own industry with global networks of interconnectivity, such as the internet.

The field of information security has developed, along with security devices such as firewalls, intrusion detection systems, and password procedures. These devices and procedures are designed to help protect organizations from the misuse and abuse that has developed along with interconnectivity and the internet. As such, business and government often use defense in-depth information assurance measures across their enterprises to plan strategically and manage IT security risks. This research study explores whether the analytical hierarchy process (AHP) model can be effectively applied to the prioritization of information assurance defense in-depth measures.

Scholar-practitioners may be interested in this research because, according to Biesecker (2010), cyber threats pose a significant risk to economic and national security. In response to these threats, the President, legislators, experts, and others have characterized cybersecurity, or measures taken to protect a computer or computer system against unauthorized access or attack, as a pressing national security issue. There is a question of whether conventional information assurance (IA) process guidance and practice, even if substantially reformed, can adequately respond to the recurrent problems and contemporary challenges of cyber-attacks (Lawrence, 2013).

Organizational computing devices are increasingly becoming targets of cyber-attacks. The organizational computing device security topic is of interest to practitioners since reporting useful findings is an important part of IT security research. Integrating relevant theory and research into IT security is also critical. According to Basagiannis, Petridou, Alexiou, Papadimitriou, and Katsaros (2011), one of the most dominant applications used by organizational computing devices is the e-mail delivery service.

Background of the Study

The background of this study involves cyber-attacks on the current information environment. Organizational computing devices are increasingly becoming targets of cyber-attacks. According to one report, "the number of cyber-attacks on organizations by outsiders is growing" (Uncertainty Abounds, 2012, p. 22).

Organizations have become dependent on the safety and security of their computer networks and their organizational computing devices. According to Stephenson (2012), securing organizational computing devices is a difficult proposition. The underlying theory of applying the AHP model to defense in-depth measures can add a different perspective to existing research and add to the information security tool kit that is available to fight cyber-attacks.

Existing research identified the growing number of cyber-attacks and the need to prevent those attacks. Blitz (2005) stated that in view of the proliferation of organizational computing devices, it is surprising how few are appropriately secured against the financial, legal, and regulatory risks associated with the potential exposure of sensitive data. Recent scholarly research regarding information security recommended that more efforts be made to secure organizational computing devices. According to the Australian Communications and Media Authority (2015), banks and credit card companies are in favor of additional security features embedded in new mobile phone payment technologies; however, there is gap in the scholarly knowledge of the need for stronger security measures.

Statement of the Problem

There are numerous organizational computing devices being used globally, and protecting these devices from criminals is becoming an increasing problem. With the growth in the amount of organizational computing devices such as the iPhone and the wealth of new Google phones, the number of organizational computing devices powerful enough to be interesting to cyber-attackers is rapidly increasing (Viega & Michael, 2010). Applying the AHP model to information assurance defense in-depth measures can give organizations scientific methods to help protect these organizational assets. Fofana (2010) reported that security controls are not associated with the appropriate information systems. The current security assessment model often results in a waste of resources, since controls that are not applicable to an information system have to be addressed.

Organizations suffer from a lack of sufficient scientific knowledge to successfully prevent cyber-attacks. Few organizations, large or small, are able to evaluate the effectiveness of the security measures they take (Uncertainty Abounds, 2012). Ongoing cyber-attacks highlight the need for a scientific investigation of the gap in information assurance research. The research problem is that information technology analysts in the United States are not using scientific methods to prioritize information assurance defense in- depth measures to protect organizational computing devices within their organizations.

Purpose of the Study

The purpose of this quantitative, non-experimental study is to examine whether or not information technology analysts are using scientific methods to prioritize information assurance defense measures in order to protect organizational computing devices in their organizations. The study was designed to investigate whether use of the Likert scale and the analytical hierarchy process can be applied to the prioritization of five information assurance defense in-

2

depth measures that are used to defend organizational computing devices against cyber-attacks. This study is essential, since exploring effective methods for preventing cyber-attacks is critical to protecting both public and private assets. In terms of information security, administrators layer their assets in defensive measures that will deter casual attackers from gaining unauthorized access (Cleghorn, 2013). Gandhi et al. (2011) reported that the study of information security becomes increasingly important in the current environment of cyber-attacks by terrorist organizations and hostile governments.

Rationale

Capturing, quantifying, and analyzing the knowledge and experience of information security analysis provides the scholarly justification for the research. This justification is from practitioner sources and is based on research that has been conducted and published in scholarly literature. Recommendations from authors for future research on improving information security methods influenced this research (Shehab & Marouf, 2012).

This study builds upon these recommendations by exploring the method of using AHP in the defense in-depth implementation process. The opinions of the sample of information technology analysts can be statistically generalizable to the entire population of information technology analysts in the United States. The results of this survey have transferability to the protection of organizational computing devices in actual organizations. According to Cooper and Schindler (2008), the ability to apply the external validity or the transferability of the findings also establishes trustworthiness in data analysis of quantitative research.

Information assurance practitioners may benefit from this research because it attempts to apply imperial research principles to the discipline of information assurance. Lawrence (2013) suggested that the problem is the inadequate and ineffective use of scientific principles, knowledge, and methods in the IA process. Cleghorn (2013, p. 144) explained that "defense in-depth is an information security practice adapted from a military defense strategy, where an attacker is forced to overcome many obstacles that eventually expend the attacker's resources".

Research Question

What is the relationship between an information technology analyst's prioritization of defense in-depth measures and the effectiveness in protecting organizational devices against cyber-attacks? Answering the research question provides value to the scholarly and practitioner information assurance communities by providing additional methods for defeating cyber-attacks. The need for quantitative solutions to defense in-depth issues helps to build a specific and detailed case to support the research questions and research methodology.

Significance of the Study

The significance of this study is that it explicitly states the value of applying AHP to scholars and practitioners who work in the field of information security. The study contributes to the body of knowledge on organizational computing security by providing both IA scholars and practitioners a scientific method for prioritizing IA measures to effectively defend organizational computing devices against cyber-attacks. It may provide a valuable addition to the existing information assurance body of knowledge.

"Layers of defense often overlap in order to ensure that internet traffic is processed multiple times by heterogeneous security technologies in hopes that the shortcomings of one security control are covered by another" (Cleghorn, 2013, p. 144). Given that academic or scholarly research builds upon itself, this research identifies the value of the application of AHP to in-depth defense results in information assurance within the scholar-practitioner community. Barnes and Barnes (2012) reported that while mobile communications were once narrowly defined by a cell phone designed for the singular purpose of telephonic convenience on-the-go, the advent of smartphone technology has moved cultural, consumer, and business sensitivities into a new era.

Definition of Terms

The following definition of terms covers the types of defense in- depth information assurance measures and related terminology encountered in IT security.

Anti-virus. Antivirus (or anti-virus) software is a class of programs that searches hard drives and floppy disks for any known or potential viruses (Harris, 2005).

Consistency index (CI). (Λ max - n)/(n - 1) gives information about logical consistency among pairwise comparison judgments in a perfect pairwise comparison case. When CI = 0.0, there is no logical inconsistency among the pairwise comparison judgments, or the judgment is considered 100% consistent (Utugizaki, Udagawa, Shinohara, & Osawa, 2007).

Consistency Ratio (CR). A measure of how consistent the judgments have been, relative to large samples of purely random judgements. If the CR is in excess of 0.1, the judgements are untrustworthy (Geoff, 2004).

Defense in-depth.

"Defense in-depth is the coordinated use of multiple security countermeasures to protect the integrity of the information assets in an enterprise. The strategy is based on the military principle that it is more difficult for an enemy to defeat a complex and multi-layered defense system than to penetrate a single barrier" (Rouse, 2007a, p. 1).

4

Effectiveness. "The degree to which objectives are achieved and the extent to which targeted problems are solved" ("Effectiveness," n.d.).

Firewall. "A firewall is a network security system, either hardware- or software-based, that controls incoming and outgoing network traffic based on a set of rules" (Cobb, 2014, p. 1).

Intrusion detection system. Host intrusion detection systems and network intrusion detection systems are methods of security management for computers and networks (Cole, 2015).

Lambda. The value equal to the number of factors in the comparison ($n = 4$) for total consistency (Alexander, 2012).

Password. "A password is an un-spaced sequence of characters used to determine that a computer user requesting access to a computer system is really that particular user" (Rouse, 2007b, p. 1).

Perceived ease of use. Perceived ease of use is the degree to which a person believes that using a particular system would be free of effort (Davis, 1989).

Smart card. A smart card is a plastic card about the size of a credit card with an embedded microchip that can be loaded with data, used for telephone calling, electronic cash payments, and other applications, and then periodically refreshed for additional use (Cobb & Meckley, 2016).

Standard cost. "An estimated or predetermined cost of performing an operation or producing a good or service, under normal conditions" ("Standard cost," n.d. p. 1).

W-vector (Eigenvectors). Eigenvectors are derived from the eigenvalues of normalized measures, i.e., the proportion of the row/column factors divided the row/column sum (Alexander, 2012).

Limitations and Assumptions

Limitations

A limitation of this research was that only registered Survey-Monkey members with the title of information technology analysts were contacted for their opinion on the defense in-depth measures. This non-experimental survey research design was used to survey a simple random sample frame of 954 active Survey-Monkey registered information technology analysts from a population of 78,020. Although there may be minor differences in the opinions of information security in different states, the opinions of the sample of information technology analysts can be statistically generalizable to the entire population of information technology analysts in the United States.

Assumptions

It was assumed that 11% ($n = 100$) of the ($n = 954$) information technology analysts random sample frame were willing to take the time and effort to open, fill out, and return the online survey. It was also assumed that the information technology analysts had the knowledge to be able to rank the five defenses in-depth information assurance measures.

Theoretical/Conceptual Framework

The best method to describe the theoretical/conceptual framework is to picture the variable interaction through the use of visualization. The framework for this study is the analytical hierarchy process (AHP) theory (Figure 1). Figure 1 also presents the interaction between AHP theory, information assurance, and resource inputs and outcomes. AHP is a decision-aiding method developed by Saaty (1994). The study's theoretical/conceptual framework, shown in Figure 1, identifies how information assurance variables interact with cost, ease of use, and effectiveness variables.

According to an Al-Harbi (2001, p. 19) article, "the goal is to quantify relative priorities for a given set of alternatives on a ratio scale, based on the judgment of the decision-maker, and stresses the importance of the intuitive judgments of a decision-maker, as well as the consistency of the comparison of alternatives in the decision-making process", using AHP methodology, a list of five information security elements was identified and their relative importance was evaluated for this research. Often, new models or theories are built by conducting scholarly research.

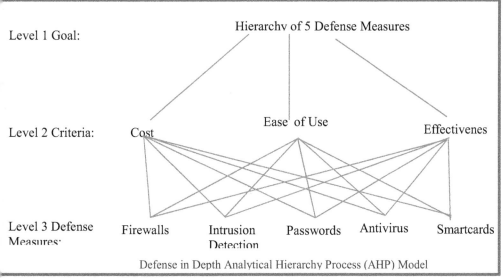

Figure 1. Hierarchy of five defense measures.

Research may be conducted to uncover what is not being addressed in the literature. Holistic pictures of an event or phenomenon are developed through the results of research. Post-positivist research is quantifiable and involves fixed, stable, observable and measurable variables.

Organization of the Remainder of the Study

This study consisted of five chapters. Chapter 2 contains 10 sections related to the historical and existing literature review. Chapter 3's sections are related to research design and methodologies used to conduct the research. Chapter 4 presents the data collection, data analyses, and results of the analyses. Finally, Chapter 5 contains the conclusions of the research and further research recommendations.

CHAPTER 2. LITERATURE REVIEW

The literature review is an organized and coherent synthesis of the best and most relevant research related to the application of AHP to organizational computing device security. It helped to define the focus of research, and this chapter provided a critical review which analyzed, critiqued, compared and contrasted a subset of both recent and seminal peer-reviewed journal articles which deal with the application of AHP theory to information assurance defense in-depth. Studies that support the dissertation's formulation of the research problem, the research question, and significance of the study are identified, described, and evaluated. The analysis of the literature also describes and evaluates studies that present the theoretical framework used to select the variables and to guide the analysis and interpretation of the data collected. Conducting a thorough literary review is an effective method for discovering ways to organize network security barriers that may have been overlooked.

Finally, the literature review identifies and explains the strengths and weaknesses of each of the articles and positions of this AHP/organizational computing device security study in a historical context. The research in this study integrates and synthesizes two areas, decision elements and the hierarchical process. The relevant theory and research reveals that AHP is an extension or expansion of logical thinking.

Historical Overview

The relevance of this literature review is that it shows the relationship of the cited works to the topic of the AHP process in relationship to organizational computing device security. The literature is organized so that the reader can perceive the relevance. It also synthesizes and evaluates studies that support the selection of the dissertation's methodology and approach. This review supports the appropriateness of the dissertation's instruments, measures, and methods used to collect data. It also defines the focus of organizational computing security research information.

According to the literature, the problems of today's population that is constantly on the move can be solved by introducing virtual organizations and organizational computing devices, such as laptops and PDAs (personal digital assistants). This chapter outlines the basics of the defense in-depth and AHP literature review. Research in the AHP process is evolutionary and new development and advances have become available over time. The study's components are organized in this chapter so that they are easily identifiable.

The literature review demonstrated the need to protect organizational computing devices that use the internet and this provides sufficient reasoning why the research questions deserve to be studied. Studies have revealed that organizational computing internet services are increasing and need to be protected. The associated services are presented as variables in the theoretical framework.

Fan (2010) posited that with the prevalence of organizational computing devices and recent advances in wireless communication technologies, organizational computing provides users with much easier access to the information and services available on the internet, regardless of users' physical locations and movement behaviors. A competency in the field of organizational computing device security was demonstrated through this review of pertinent scholarly and practitioner literature. Mobile organizational computing removes the restrictions of time and location.

The literature review presents a thorough review of the literature and relevant research findings to support the research questions, theoretical underpinnings, and methodological design choices. According to de Reuver, Bouwman, Prieto, and Visser (2011), development of advanced mobile internet services requires flexible service platforms. The cohesive and integrated analysis of existing research literature presents a balanced picture on the need for flexible defense platforms.

Recent literature explained that workers are performing their duties from numerous locations. By integrating what has been written about organizational computing device defenses into a sufficient set of logical reasons, a case can be made for why further research is needed. Liu (2010) stated that mobile workers are away from their desks regularly and use organizational computing devices in various locations to perform their duties.

This review of defense in-depth literature is organized according to Bloom's taxonomy (Armstrong, n.d.), which describes how knowledge is acquired, used, transformed, and evaluated. These services are also the focus for this research and guide the analysis and interpretation of the data collected. Knowledge on organizational computing defense security is acquired based on the information contained within this review. That knowledge was then conveyed and applied through the results of the study.

Barnes and Barnes (2012) stated that while mobile communications were once narrowly defined as a cell phone designed for the singular purpose of telephonic convenience on-the-go, the advent of smartphone technology moved cultural, consumer, and business sensitivities into a new era. This review of network defense in-depth and AHP focuses on explaining, integrating, and coordinating information which is both integrated and conclusive. The literature is organized in clusters of relationships, grouped around major themes or topics, and selected from diverse and relevant sources.

The need for increased network security, as outlined in the literature, provides sufficient reasons for advancing the knowledge and supporting research objectives. Research explains the importance of security measures to mobile communications. This supports the appropriateness of the instruments, measures, and methods used to collect data in this study.

Vogt (2007) stated that it is impossible to think about any moderately complex research problem without using both quantitative and qualitative reasoning. This review of defense in-depth and AHP provide a historical perspective, which introduces the work of seminal authors and built on their research and associated studies that support the research. The literature shows the relevance of research done with both quantitative and qualitative research methods so that future researchers can choose which method is most appropriate for the research that they are doing.

The defense in-depth and AHP literature begins with the theoretical development and its implications on both scholarly research and practitioner application. AHP is a multiple criteria decision-making tool (Vaidya & Kumar, 2006). According to the literature, most forms of decision-making involve some part of AHP.

Recent and seminal peer reviewed AHP articles explain that AHP is both a decision making and research tool. Defense in-depth and AHP articles are outlined and assembled in a logical order that support the goals of this research. Practitioners, such as financial analysts, have used AHP as a decision making tool since its inception.

A thorough review of the literature shows that AHP can be used in many different ways. This review upholds the intent of the defense in-depth scholarly and practitioner articles, comprehending the knowledge content that they contained within. Finally, this review of the literature explains both the parameters of the review and the basis for selecting the literature included. It also identifies highlights and key information content. Evaluation of recent studies has identified the need to enhance security for organizational computing devices. During this review, primary sources were used whenever possible.

Defense In-Depth

An understanding of the key literary contributors and their contribution reveals that there are no simple solutions to network security. According to Brooke (2001), network security continues to grow more complex. Seminal literature on network security and defense in-depth are relevant resources with regard to the dissertation topic.

According to Bakolas and Saleh (2011) defense in-depth is a fundamental principle/strategy for achieving system safety. An analytical process is absent in the application of defense in-depth theory. The lack of quantitative analytical research on defense in-depth applications represents a gap in the existing research.

The defense in-depth literature revealed that one set of centralized network security measures cannot be applied to current networks. Services that once were centralized and available to a relatively small group of internal users are becoming decentralized and available to a wide audience via the internet and extranet (Brooke, 2001). Implications in recent articles such as Brooke's stated that a decentralized solution is needed. A detailed summary of defense in-depth articles, as they relate to this research, revealed that current networks are multi-layered.

10

For many organizations, the audience now comprises users within the enterprise, as well as customers, business partners, and prospects beyond traditional network boundaries (Brooke, 2001). Cost savings through the use of defense in-depth measures are shown in cohesive research results reports. The network security article by Brooke documented the need for defense in-depth and is germane to the dissertation study. This cost savings, through added protection, helps to build a case to support the research.

Defense in-depth is the practice of layering defenses to provide added protection. Defense in-depth increases security by raising the cost of an attack (Brooke, 2001). Revealing knowledge on how to raise the cost of cyberattacks for intruders provides an argument that validates this research's objectives. The Brooke article helps to explore and clarify the project's scope and objective of prioritizing defense in-depth measures.

The need to organize barriers against cyber-attacks, as described in the literature, provided a case for how this research builds on the current literature. This system places multiple barriers between an attacker and business-critical information resources. The deeper an attacker tries to go, the harder it gets (Brooke, 2001).

The research methodology of analytically prioritizing multiple barriers supports the research purpose. A summary of significant results and implications of in-depth research reveals that defense in-depth measures can also help to reduce network surveillance. This research is an argument that supports the theoretical defense in-depth base. These multiple layers prevent direct attacks against important systems and avert easy reconnaissance of networks (Brooke, 2001). Practical application of defense in-depth measures, as outlined by the literature, applies directly to the purpose of this research.

Brooke's (2001) seminal article presented an in-depth exploration of the theoretical underpinning of multilayered defense through a careful analysis, evaluation, and integration. Information security research is also tied to ongoing research in strategic organizational planning and policy implementation. Johna (2004) stated that defense-in-depth lets IT executives more effectively tie their network security strategies into the overall organizational information stewardship policy.

A report by Johna (2004) supported the defense in-depth research objectives. It also helped to synthesis the existing network security body of knowledge. Johna's seminal article explained how existing research increases understanding of the need for defense in-depth. To create an effective defense-in-depth strategy, IT executives need an architectural structure that intelligently grants permission to applications, data, and resources (Johna, 2004). Information on defense in-depth measures is acquired and categorized in a logical manner. Further, Johna acknowledged significant previous research on defense-in-depth strategy and theory.

11

Research results (Brooke, 2001; Johna, 2004) have shown that the use of defense in-depth measures is an important part of information assurance stewardship. Network managers should reassess their security architectures in the overall context of information stewardship – and enabling defense-in-depth is a great first step. Johna (2004) provided indirect support for this study's research questions and methodology.

Network security architectures efforts are described by Johna (2004), whose argument reflects a depth of understanding, a coordination of facts, results, and conclusions that interpret and substantiate the research objective. Defense-in-depth lets IT executives more effectively tie their network security strategies into the overall organizational information stewardship policy. The research objective of using AHP to prioritize defense in-depth measures are coordinated with existing permission granting theory as explained by Johna.

The objective is analysis and synthesis to evaluate the results and determine the potential for expanding the existing knowledge base. Valid policy information on the defense in-depth topic is presented by Johna (2004). Information offered by Johna aligns with the chosen research design and with the research questions. This scholarly literature, along with additional articles on defense in-depth, has a direct influence on this study.

This combined set of published literature represents an important part of the existing knowledge base about defense in-depth. A multi-layered defense strategy is the result of reasoning and logic used for selecting the elements (passwords, encryption, smart-cards and firewalls) of the research design, as described by Hoff (2004). Hoff (2004) also explained that security in storage networks can only be achieved by a strategy that is multi-layered and that meets company specific requirements.

The multi-layered theory is the reasoning behind the choice of the AHP data analysis procedure. Hoff (2004) explained the proposed dissertation study in a broader scholarly literature base by stating the importance of layered defense. The multiple lines of defense that Hoff described helped to address the study's research questions. The defense in-depth strategy is a layered architecture where different security technologies are deployed on top of each other to implement multiple lines of defense.

Empirical and theoretical issues relevant to defense in-depth are discussed in the Mazu Networks (2005) press release. The rationale for the use of the chosen research design is that some companies are uncertain how to prioritize defense in-depth measures. The research notes that although companies today are clearly more educated on the risks associated with an open network, they are still uncertain as to what steps are needed to protect their critical assets from compromise. The study's information technology analysts sampling frame helped to provide critical knowledge to address these security uncertainties.

Exploring critical defense in-depth issues provide significant contributions to the scholarship of network security. A need for a complete defense in-depth strategy, as outlined in Mazu Networks (2005), supported recommendations for future research. While security technologies, including firewalls, IDS/IPS devices and security event management tools remain essential, a complete defense-in-depth strategy within today's complex security environment demands protection at the internal network level.

This dissertation study's participant selection process and analytical techniques were derived from the need to prioritize constructs such as firewalls and IDS/IPS devices discussed in the Mazu Networks (2005) information, which provided relevant findings on network management tools that pertain to leadership, human resources, general business and information security. An in-depth analysis of Mazu Networks' and other articles were used to evaluate the content in relation to this study. Bond (2004) also contributed to the existing body of data center security knowledge and practices.

An explanation of the relationship between defense in-depth and business strategy offered by Bond (2004) demonstrated a depth of understanding that is both integrated and conclusive. The author stated that aligning this security policy to business goals will help to define security zones, which are areas of the data center separated to minimize the impact of an attack. The use of security posture assessments is directly related to this study's design since Bond extended the network security and business integration frontier of knowledge. Following this up with a security posture assessment allows a business to set appropriate risk levels for each zone based on importance and cost.

An alternative interpretation to the existing understanding of perimeter security, prioritizing security throughout the network, as explained by Bond (2004), is a core theory which formed the base of this study's research phenomena. At the heart of the process should be a strategy of defense in-depth, not just securing the perimeter or deploying some access controls internally. According to Bond, placing security throughout the network to defend the storage area network (SAN) so there are layers of security before a malicious program or hacker can reach the crown jewels is an appropriate strategy.

The Bond (2004) article offered a scholar-practitioner framework that addressed the advantages of defense in-depth in SAN networks. Ineffective and isolated defenses, as outlined by Luallen and Hamburg (2009), are important in defining the focus of research. Significant network security weaknesses and practical alternatives are discussed in the Luallen and Hamburg article.

Luallen and Hamburg (2009) explained that one of the most important realizations cyber security engineers made in their early work is that security efforts are ineffective in isolation. The need to develop information assurance as a coordinated effort, and not in isolation, as outlined in this article forms the AHP theoretical framework used to guide the study and to guide the analysis and interpretation of the data collected. The study of the application of the AHP to defense in-depth measures could impact some of network weaknesses as discussed by Luallen and Hamburg (2009).

This article explanation of multiple and varying defense in-depth methods support the selection of this study's methodology and approach. It was this vital realization that gave birth to the concept of defense-in-depth, which is a technique of defending systems against any particular attack vector using multiple and varying methods (Luallen & Hamburg, 2009). The use of national security professionals in this article supports the appropriateness of this study's methods used to collect data, which is polling security professionals.

This article proposes a network security approach which addresses security problems faced by national security organizations. Measures used to collect data are supported by the layering strategy as outlined in this article. Documented historically by Sun Tzu and re-conceived by the National Security Agency, this layering strategy aims at providing a comprehensive approach to information and electronic security (Luallen & Hamburg, 2009).

The number of different types of threats that face networks and the need to defeat those threats as outlined in this article supports the research questions, theoretical underpinnings, and methodological design choices. The need for defense in-depth on networks at various levels of civil society and government are discussed in the article. A cohesive and integrated analysis of this existing research presents one viewpoint among various scholarly viewpoints on the number and type of threats facing information assurance organizations.

While many industrial control systems are becoming commercially available with various integrated cyber security controls, the reality is these systems are still susceptible to many types of threats (Luallen & Hamburg, 2009). The question of how to deploy defense in-depth measures as outlined in this article adds to the set of logical reasons for why further research is needed. The article explained how research on defense in-depth techniques responds to the problem of network security and provides new knowledge by which to better deal with the problem.

The question of how to maximize security defenses, as asked in this article, provides a competent and sufficient rationale for the research question posed in Chapter 1. The question that system owners and implementers raise was "How do we maximize the assurance that our industrial control systems will be sufficiently resilient against cyber-attacks once deployed? The answer is defense-in-depth" (Luallen & Hamburg, 2009, p. 30). This article reported how information assurance knowledge is acquired, used, transformed, and evaluated.

The degree to which defense in-depth research is of interest to the scholarly community and outside groups is clearly explained in the article by Luallen and Hamburg (2009). Knowledge of redundant network defense is acquired based on the information contained within a Jackson (2004) article and how that knowledge is conveyed and applied. The

14

understanding of network security integrity, as explained in this Jackson research article, may help to challenge and prepare the reader to assume his or her role as a professional in the field.

Jackson (2004) clarified that absolute network integrity is vital to protect Office of Naval Intelligence (ONI) operations, according to George M. Barton, deputy director of ONI's Information Technology Directorate. Jackson (2004) set the stage for subsequent sections in this study by evaluating previous network security research methods and failures and by providing a framework for formulating future research design and methods. Jackson's explanation on eliminating single points of failure displays the importance of integrating and coordinating security information which demonstrates a depth of understanding that is both integrated and conclusive. ONI relies on a range of protections so that there is no one point of failure on its six networks (Jackson, 2004). "'I want overlap, I want redundancy,' Barton said. 'I want automatic systems, I want manual systems. There is value in all of that'" (Jackson, 2004, p. 15). This article helps to serve as a benchmark for comparing the results of this study with those found in the defense in-depth literature.

The need for analytical redundant security, as outlined in this literature review, provides sufficient reasons for advancing the knowledge and supporting the research objective. A thorough scrutiny of the existing literature shows that a complex solution is needed to protect networks from cyber-attacks. The complexity of current networks and the need to protect them as outlined in this review help to build a specific and detailed "case" to support the research questions and research methodology.

According to Huntley's (2010) wording in a real-time world, today's reality is that day-to-day business demands require a complex web of connectivity between customers, agencies, carriers, and managing general agents that can leave critical data susceptible to unauthorized access. The Huntley article builds on the work of seminal authors and on their research of defense in-depth topics. The work also supports the research questions and the choice of methodology.

The need to integrate and synthesize layers of network defense is explained in this Huntley (2010) article. Achieving these goals requires more than use of complicated passwords and isolated networks with firewalls. According to the article, defense in-depth and building a perimeter around network resources begins with the theoretical development and its implications on both scholarly research and practitioner application.

Huntley (2010) documented a conceptual debate between single layered versus multilayered defense. A historical approach is chosen in this literature review and it outlines those articles and assembles them in a logical order that supports the goals of this defense in-depth prioritization research. Huntly posited that mmaintaining CIA takes vigilant maintenance of security measures at every layer, combined with implementing a defense in-depth strategy that puts controls around user workstations, the network's perimeter, internal network, host systems, applications, system interfaces, and databases.

Key information content components are outlined in this Huntley (2010) article. A critical and relevant review of recent literature continues to support the fundamental need for defense in-depth. The identification of defense in-depth fundamentals is a key contribution to defense in-depth theory (Bakolas & Saleh, 2011).

According to Bakolas and Saleh (2011) defense in-depth is a fundamental principle/strategy for achieving system safety. An analytical process is absent in the application of defense in-depth theory. The lack of quantitative analytical research on defense in-depth applications represents a gap in the existing research.

The results, conclusions, and implications in this research calls for redundant and multilayered defenses to protect network resources.

> "First conceptualized within the nuclear industry, defense-in-depth is the basis for risk-informed decisions by the U.S. Nuclear Regulatory Commission, and is recognized under various names in other industries e.g., layers of protection in the chemical industry" (Bakolas & Saleh, 2011, p. 184).

A detailed summary of the article as it relates to this study reveals that accidents and breaches of defenses can be avoided through a multilayered approach.

The Bakolas and Saleh (2011) article introduced risk informed decisions as a viable defense in-depth research design and methodology. Bakolas and Saleh found that accidents typically result from the absence or breach of defenses or violation of safety constraints. A cohesive report of the results in this article shows that defense in-depth involves a diversified set of defense measures.

This quantitative research study helped to bridge the gap between risk-based decision making and the analytical application of defense in-depth measures. The organization of multiple defense measures to protect networks as outlined in this research supports the objective of this quantitative study. It also leads to a greater understanding of the multilayered defense phenomenon.

Defense-in-depth is realized by a diversity of safety barriers and a network of redundancies (Bakolas & Saleh, 2011). The explanation of the need for diverse barriers is an argument that the article validates the study's research objective. Recent defense in-depth literature review reveals a need to use a diverse set of defense measures which is the theoretical and/or conceptual context for the dissertation study.

The number of recent cyber-attacks as outlined in the Warner (2013) article builds on the need for further research that this study provides. An awareness of types of cyber-attacks and how to defeat them is important theoretical

16

and research/methodological developments in the defense in-depth specialization. Warner stated that in 2011, over 100,000 cyber-attacks occurred against U.S. government and commercial networks.

A description of Warner's (2013) research methodology explained that intruders are forced to defeat one layer of defense after the other with the use of defense in-depth. This argument supports the purpose and theoretical base of this quantitative study. A summary of significant results and implications of this research explains the confidence that the US military has in the use of defense in-depth theory.

Many types of malware specifically target control systems. To combat such attacks, the military requires a defense-in-depth (DID) strategy (Warner, 2013). Articles related to the U.S. military use of defense in-depth measures identifies some of the most pertinent and relevant literature to the proposed study. This article described a U.S. military practitioner application of defense in-depth as it applies to the purpose of this study.

A concise synthesis of the findings revealed the improvement in network defense through the use of defense in-depth measures. This study also ties in to ongoing research in parallel defense which is a related field. DID consists of several layers of both physical and cyber safeguards for a given system, forcing the attacker to penetrate a first layer of defense and also a back-up layer and so on (Warner, 2013).

A summary of this article states that the failure of one defense measure can be supported by the success of another measure which supported this study's research objective. This relevant Warner (2013) article highlights the military use of defense in-depth measures. This information in this article helps to acquire U.S. military defense in-depth knowledge and categorize it in a logical manner.

In describing DID, Jeff Johnson, Command Information Officer for Naval District Washington, says, "It's important in order to make sure that one of the attack vectors or all of the attack vectors can be mitigated kind of in parallel" (Warner, 2013, p. 30). A characterization of the results of this study reveals an integration of defense in-depth into an organization's overall defense strategy: "We look at defense in-depth as part of an overall strategy associated with our infrastructure" (Warner, 2013, p. 31).

This source provided an indirect support for the study's research question and methodology. This literary review helps to distinguish among different types of defense in-depth literature; one type is the original seminal literature which covers the beginning use of defense in-depth measures for network defense and the more recent literature. The network security results listed in Warner's (2013) article can be used as a building block as part of the scholarly research for this study.

Wireless networking device vendors are meeting the challenge of offering equipment that can protect sensitive military and industrial control networks from many types of attack while presenting a defense-in-depth approach to network security (Warner, 2013). The methodology used in the article aligns with the research question. Both seminal and recent literature that covers defense in-depth application and theory are appropriate for this study. The defense in-depth efforts from vendors, military and industry in this article directly influence the design of this quantitative study.

Advanced Persistent Threats (APT)

According to Cleghorn (2013), defense against persistent attacks is a limitation to defense in-depth. The article uses a multitude of measures and across different settings and populations to point out differences between the two network defense theories. Recommendations and implications for future research are to improve defense in-depth so that is more effective against persistent attacks, which is a justification for this study.

A substantial portion of this paper's body is devoted to comparing real-world usage scenarios and discussing the flaws in each method (Cleghorn, 2013). The research question of whether AHP can be used to prioritize defense in-depth measures is linked to the theoretical framework of protection against persistent attacks. The need for defense measures which can defeat persistent as well as a large number of attacks are conclusions addressed in this study, the study also addressed recommendations for future research.

A well-tuned defense in-depth architecture will prevent a vast majority of attacks and alert an administrator to intrusions that pass through (Cleghorn, 2013). Problems faced by persistent attacks and recommendations for future research, as outlined in this article, are elements of interest and are addressed in the study. However, according to Cleghorn, persistent attacks can present a problem for network defenses that use defense in-depth measures.

An in-depth analysis of this article revealed that persistent attacks represent a new type of threat, advanced persistent threats (APT) provides an entirely new challenge to administrators, who now have to face organized attackers with resources and motivation that have never been seen before (Cleghorn, 2013). The threats of persistent attacks to networks as outlined in this article are both integrated and conclusive. These types of attacks will influence defense in-depth theory.

The APT material presented in this article helps to justify the need for and interest in conducting the proposed research on the analytical use of defense in-depth measures. Recent literature reveals different framed APT hypotheses which analytical defense in-depth procedures can effectively address. The existence of APT helps to build a case from the research to support this study.

Moon, Im, Lee, and Park (2014) explained that APT use malware for the purpose of leaking the data of large corporations and government agencies. Analysis and findings are organized in this research by Moon et al. (2014) in a way which aids in the formulation of defense in-depth theory.

APT attacks target systems continuously by utilizing intelligent and complex technologies (Moon et al., 2014). This recent article helps to further establish the rationale for the study and establishes the way—methodologically—in which others have approached defense in-depth problems. This article on how threats attempt to defeat network defenses supports a case for how the literature builds on this study.

To overthrow the elaborate security network of target systems, it conducts an attack after undergoing a pre-reconnaissance phase. An APT attack causes financial loss, information leakage, and so on (Moon et al., 2014). Moon et al.'s article accomplishes the goal of identifying how this quantitative study fits into and contributes to the existing literature on defeating APT cyber-attacks.

A short description of this article outlines a defense in-depth approach to defeat APTs and it is supported by the purpose of this study. They can easily bypass the antivirus system of a target system. In this quantitative study, we propose a multi-layer defense system (MLDS) that can defend against APT (Moon et al., 2014). This study may extend the previous work done by Moon et al. on understanding and preventing APT attacks. The assertion that APT attacks can be defeated by defense in-depth measures is a summary of significant results and implications of this research. Failure to develop methods for organizing defense in-depth measures is one of the limitations of the previous research and provides solid justification for further research on this topic.

Defense in-Breadth Argument

A broad review of defense in-depth theory provides a substantial base of theoretical knowledge and compares and contrasts competing views. The population and sampling strategy of this study was designed to explore competing theories to defense in-depth. One competing theory is defense in breadth versus defense in-depth.

According to Cleghorn (2013), the defense in-depth methodology was popularized in the early 2000's amid growing concerns for information security. The reasoning behind the data collection procedures and choice of data analysis tools is to remedy some of the defense in-depth shortcomings. Cleghorn's article points out experimental empirical results to a network defense theory which counters some defense in-depth weaknesses.

Cleghorn's (2013) article outlines some of the arguments against the defense in-depth argument. In the last two years, many supporters of the defense in-depth security methodology have changed their allegiance to an offshoot method dubbed the defense in breadth methodology. An effective review and critique of both theories is presented in the article.

Evaluating a defense in-depth approach that can overcome a number of different attacks is a rationale for the use of the chosen research design. Defense in-depth is an information security practice adapted from a military defense strategy where an attacker is forced to overcome a great many obstacles that eventually expend the attacker's resources (Cleghorn, 2013). The security analysis population, sampling frame, and sampling strategy was chosen for their ability to respond to security alerts, which is outlined as a critical network defense component in this article.

A finding of the article is that an effective deployment of defense in-depth measures will stop most forms of cyber-attacks. Scholarly research on the proper use of defense in-depth measures is directly related to the design of this research study. Improperly deployed, the defense in-depth architecture weakens the human component and makes this system difficult to maintain (Cleghorn, 2013).

Cleghorn's (2013) article from the academic literature is representative of the key author's writing and research in the field of information assurance and is peer-reviewed. An in-depth analysis of the critical literature highlights the seeming paradoxes and contradictions in the existing literature on both of these network defense theories. The defense in-depth architecture concedes several points inherently that are worth noting as many criticisms of the methodology focus on these concessions.

Cleghorn's (2013) article helps to support the dissertation's formulation of the research problem, the research question, and significance of the study. Critics of the defense in-depth theory claim within the literature that defense in-depth measures will fail overtime during an APT. Organizing defense in-depth measures so that they will defeat attacks overtime, as outlined in this article is the theoretical framework used to select the variables for the study and it guides the analysis and interpretation of the data collected.

The architecture concedes that attacks will occur, and given enough time, these attacks will begin to circumvent security controls (Cleghorn, 2013). A synthesis and evaluation of the article supports the selection of the dissertation's methodology and approach. This study underlined the potential contribution to the resolution of the conceptual arguments along with a better understanding of this network defense phenomenon.

The use of security analysis is an appropriate method used to collect data for this study because of their involvement in the information security community. Defense in breadth is a methodology that came about suddenly with little legitimate acknowledgement in the information security community (Cleghorn, 2013). The counter arguments in this article assisted in organizing thinking about the literature review and how to present the results.

Every dissertation sets out to achieve some worthy cause and making defense in-depth theory and practice more effective against APT, for example, can potentially fill a gap in the existing literature. Defense in breath is highlighted as not a fully developed theory in this article and key information content is missing. Rather than a fully developed methodology, defense in breadth appears to just be a patch for the defense in-depth architecture already in place that promises to fix the issues without addressing the root causes (Cleghorn, 2013).

Cleghorn's (2013) article is a key contribution to the continued development of defense in breadth theory. Defense in-depth knowledge and information that addresses the root causes and prevention of cyber-attacks are missing or unknown about the phenomenon in the existing literature. The theory and application of defense in breadth are solid according to this article and they run parallel to defense in-depth theory and application.

Aspects of the defense in breadth methodology are sound; however, the similarities to the defense in-depth method are apparent (Cleghorn, 2013). The research results, conclusions, and implications are much the same among the two theories. This critical review of the literature further uncovers gaps between the interaction between defense in-depth and defense in breadth theories.

This study has the potential to help fill those gaps. The founding principal of defense in breadth is layering heterogeneous security technologies in the common attack vectors to ensure that attacks missed by one technology are caught by another (Cleghorn, 2013). A detailed summary of the article as it relates to the research reveals that defense in breadth is another component which can be added to network defense. Cleghorn (2013) helped to provide insights to various methodological considerations for the study.

Hirschmann (2014) stated that a multi-layered defense in-depth strategy helps organizations address many of the most common causes of breaches. This previous work identified a gap in determining an effective method for prioritizing defense in-depth measures. Mobile end-points are susceptible to malware and malicious attacks, particularly when devices are used outside the safe confines of the immediate corporate network. By addressing the organizational computing device security findings that are outlined in this article, this quantitative study contribute to the incremental accumulation of scientific knowledge on the organizational computing device security topic.

Even as the "Bring Your Own Device" trend and the "Internet of Things" trend increase the number of mobile endpoints in corporate settings, defense in-depth, network, and security components providing redundancy and constant communication lessens the chance these devices will become exploitable vulnerabilities (Hirschmann, 2014). This quantitative study contributes to theory and practice within the organizational computing device security specialization by recommending an effective method for deploying defense in-depth measures. The first step of a defense in-depth strategy to protect against network breaches should be to establish proper access control systems. By recommending a method for determining appropriate access controls, this quantitative study improves the ability of the scholar-practitioner to be an effective leader, helping professional, and agent for change.

Before granting access rights, an enterprise's system should check whether users have the correct device identities, such as software, hardware, and network attributes and user identities for each individual attribute of a user (Hirschmann, 2014). The Hirschmann article explained the need to add analytical defense in-depth procedures to the existing body of knowledge and theoretical defense in-depth frameworks. Network and security components must be able to communicate so that if an attacker penetrates one system, others can respond immediately to take preventative measures. According to this article, defense in-depth measures that communicate and interact represent the best practices in the field.

Appropriate defense in-depth procedures represent a solution of problems encountered in the field, according to Byres (2014). According to Byres, cybersecurity-related events have become an increasing problem for the oil and gas industry over the past decade. An analytical determination of defense in-depth procedures represents innovations and improvements in the field of network security and risk management. Ultimately, these circumstances are leading to a do-or-die moment: either secures your individual computer systems or the reliability and safety of your entire company is at risk.

Subsequent research may advance theory of defense in-depth and help to protect companies in the field. Of course, there's no simple solution–the process takes substantial effort and thorough planning (Byres, 2014). Byres revealed internal oil industry reports that provide indications of professional or practical concerns about cyber-attacks and protection outcomes. A carefully constructed and strategically designed defense in-depth model is the only viable answer. This article explains that defense in-depth should also work within the institution's agenda and should be handled with care.

Founding of Analytical Hierarchy Process (AHP) Theory

This review of AHP literature summarizes the gathered AHP knowledge into a cohesive argument that reflects a depth of understanding, a coordination of facts, results. Wind and Saaty (1980) focused on the founding and versatility of the AHP theory. According to this article, a comparison can be made between any person, thing, or situation.

Wind and Saaty (1980) makes more assertions about AHP than do the other articles. This is an argument that supports the theoretical base of the study. According to Wind and Saaty, the analytic hierarchy process (AHP) structures any complex, multi-person, multi-period, multi-criterion problem hierarchically. The Wind and Saaty (1980) article's explanation of AHP multi-criterion problem solving characteristics can be used for defense in-depth practitioner applications as they apply to the purpose of this study. Strength of this seminal article is that it describes how elements of the AHP process are weighted at each level of the hierarchy. The other seminal articles focused less on the weighted elements.

A summary of the articles support the study's defense in-depth prioritization objective. According to Wind and Saaty (1980), using a method for scaling the weights of the elements in each level of the hierarchy with respect to an element of the next higher level, a matrix of pairwise comparisons of the activities can be constructed. A subset of both recent and seminal reveals that the results of the measured elements are aligned in a matrix. The matrix research design (methodology) listed in this article is aligned with the research questions. AHP starts by decomposing a complex problem into a hierarchy (Wind & Saaty, 1980). This article describes AHP's problem diagnosis synthesis process.

A measurement methodology is used to establish priorities among the elements within each stratum of the hierarchy (Wind & Saaty, 1980). The AHP model has not been extensively applied to defense in-depth which is one of the limitations of the research. Seminal research describes the research method of comparison at each level of the hierarchy.

Relevant theory and research articles explain the integration of the comparisons hieratically. This seminal article focuses more on the AHP process and less on AHP application in comparison to the recent articles. The pair comparison matrices that are described in this study sufficiently addressed the research question.

Structurally, the hierarchy is broken down into a series of pair comparison matrices, and the participants were asked to evaluate the off-diagonal relationship in one half of each matrix (Wind & Saaty, 1980). This article synthesizes the off-diagonal relationship portion of the AHP theory. This relationship is not often emphasized in the literature.

The strength of Wind and Saaty (1980) is that integrates the relevance of hierarchical pair comparisons. This article similar to the other articles focuses AHP's pair wise comparisons. Each pair is evaluated separately as to the degree to which one item of a pair dominates the other with respect to the elements from the next level in the hierarchy.

The Solving of Complex Problems

The theoretical framework in Saaty (1994) is linked to the explanation of AHP processes. The seminal articles point out the essential AHP components and processes. The AHP comparison components provide the rationale for the use of the chosen research design.

The more recent articles focus less on these components. According to Saaty (1994) the analytic hierarchy process (AHP) includes both the rating and comparison methods. The population and sampling strategy for this research is designed rating and comparing specific defense in-depth measures. The Saaty seminal article points out that AHP consist of ratings and comparisons. The other articles failed to point this out. This seminal article also includes practical elements that are still applicable.

The strength of Saaty's (1994) article is that it provides greater detail about decision elements and hierarchy in contrast to the other articles. The reliable hierarchic structure that is described by Saaty supported the analytical/statistical methods used in this research. Rationality requires developing a reliable hierarchic structure or feedback network that includes criteria of various types of influence, stakeholders, and decision alternatives to determine the best choice.

An in-depth analysis and sufficient detail in the Saaty (1994) article helps to link the AHP process to the interconnections of defense in-depth measures as they relate to this research. Traditional logical thinking leads to sequences of ideas that are so tangled that their interconnections are not readily discerned. This article points out that AHP gives the practitioner the opportunity to see complex problems and with more focus.

Saaty (1994) laid out both the short-term and long-term comparison of alternatives which demonstrates a depth of understanding that is both integrated and conclusive. The other articles do not make this clear. Saaty outlined the problem AHP is designed to solve. Saaty (1994) explained the core theory, which forms the root of the research phenomena for the study. The other articles focused less on how AHP was developed. A way to determine which objective outweighs another is needed, both in the near and long terms.

A last and often crucial disadvantage of many traditional decision-making methods is that they require specialized expertise to design the appropriate structure, and then to embed the decision-making process in it (Saaty, 1994). The requirement for an appropriate evaluation structure is a highlight of the key information content of this article. The strength of this article is that it warns the reader of potential AHP flaws.

A synthesis of relevant theory and research revealed that a number of decision-making processes suffer from the same weakness. The Saaty (1994) articles explanation for developing an appropriate comparison structure for decision making helped to build a case from the research to support this quantitative study. The Saaty article described both AHP's strength and weaknesses in comparison to the other articles that only point out the strength of the process.

Saaty's (1994) research is a key contribution to the AHP field and formed the basis for the methodology used in this study. The AHP is about breaking a problem down and then aggregating the solutions of all the sub-problems into a conclusion. Finally, this article describes the overall AHP concept. This study explores whether AHP theory can be used in the practical application of defense in-depth measures. A synthesis of relevant theory and research discusses the breakdown of an aggregate problem into individual pieces, and then the development of an aggregate solution to the problem.

Processing Alternatives

Implications from having the ability to narrow down a set of defense in-depth alternatives are the focus of this study. According to Sedzro, Marouane, and Assogbavi (2012) in the AHP process, a set of alternatives and constraints are narrowed down. A detailed summary of the article describes the process of evaluating more than two alternatives which may be applied to defense in-depth as it relates to the research.

The AHP process weeds out alternatives and makes a group of best alternatives, or identifies one alternative clearer than the others. This is a slightly different approach to AHP than is outlined in the other articles. In terms of asset management, AHP must take into consideration a number of different factors, such as market atmosphere and investor attitudes.

Sedzro et al. (2012) reported the results of multi-criteria decision-making in a cohesive manner. An application of relevant theory and research reveals that AHP can be used for marketing and investment decisions. The AHP theory can go beyond the two-criterion decision making process, which can lead to the optimization method that traditionally prevails in the financial literature (Sedzro et al., 2012).

The Sedzro et al. (2012) article focus on investment applications is an argument that it supports the research objective. Strength of this recent article is that it discusses AHP's ability to deal with multi-criteria when it comes to investments applications. This recent Sedzro et al. (2012) article relayed an understanding of AHPs ability to go beyond the investor two-criterion decision model and its ability to employ research methods to handle complex investment decisions.

The integrated asset management focus of the Sedzro et al. (2012, p. 96) article makes a case for how the literature builds on this quantitative study. "This recent article suggests a procedure that makes integrated asset management possible, based on the analytic hierarchy process, combined with a mean variance and goal programming model." Practitioners combine AHP with additional models to enhance their decision-making process. Development is logical and clear in the practical use of AHP in portfolio management.

The research methodology in the Sedzro et al. (2012) article which evaluated multiple criteria simultaneously supports the study's purpose. The evaluation of recent research points out that AHP is linked appropriately in the field of asset management. This recent article describes the integration of AHP, mean variance, and goal programming.

The results of AHP outperforming the Standard and Poors (S&P) index as described in Sedzro et al. (2012) can have implications for defense in-depth application. The results obtained are encouraging, as the portfolios constructed in this manner perform better than the S&P index. The AHP managed portfolios often outperform certain market indexes. Saaty's (1994) description of logical consistency within AHP also provided an argument for practitioner applications as it applies to the purpose of the research. The strength of this article is that it showed actual successes of practical AHP use for investing.

According to Sedzro et al. (2012), AHP relevant theory and research is applied to actual stock markets. The author explained a multi-criteria form of investing. A summary of individual rating and comparison, as outlined in Sedzro et al. supports the research objective. A thorough review of the literature points out that the practical use of AHP to balance an investors, goals and wealth with market conditions. Developed by Saaty (1980), the AHP is a technique used for dealing with complex, unstructured problems (Sedzro et al., 2012). The theory allows for the evaluation of multiple criteria simultaneously.

The AHP hierarchization of elements, as summarized in the literature, provides direct support for the research questions and methodology. The Sedzro et al. (2012) article uses Saaty's (1980) theory to effectively make decisions in a complicated modern stock market. It is based on three principles: hierarchization, priority-setting, and logical consistency.

Sedzro et al. (2012) defined three basic AHP principles. Elements are placed in logical order, priorities are set, and the elements are rated against each other. Sedzro et al. provided a consistency index which summarized knowledge into a cohesive argument that reflects a depth of understanding, a coordination of facts, results, and conclusions that interpret and substantiated the research objective.

According to Sedzro et al. (2012), AHP effectively employs the research methods of hierarchization, priority-setting, and logical consistency. An application of relevant AHP theory and research hierarchization is outlined in this recent article. Differences in AHP elements are synthesized using weights according to this recent article.

The comparison research design which is outlined in Sedzro et al. (2012) is aligned with the research questions. This recent article focused more on priority settings than do the other articles. Although AHP is a systematic form of prioritization, some results are subjective. As this recent article points out, a weakness of AHP is that the AHP pairing is sometimes subjective.

The method of using judgement systematically in the Sedzro et al. (2012) scholarly article directly influences this study. An understanding of AHP theory reveals that not all of its results are objective. The AHP method uses a consistency index that enables to test the consistency of judgments systematically. The consistency index can reduce the level of human bias in studies and increase its validity and reliability.

The logical and consistent AHP methods that are described in Sedzro et al. (2012) are reasons selecting the elements of the research design. The information security analysis population may be able to use these methods to deploy defense in-depth measures. According to the AHP theory as outlined in the recent Sedzro et al. article, AHP includes a development that logically and clearly measures consistency.

The consistency index, as described in Sedzro et al. (2012), helps to eliminate judgmental pairing. This strengthens the theory and helps to eliminate research bias. For example, if A is considered five times preferable to B, and B is twice as preferable as C, than A must be considered 10 times preferable to C. Otherwise, the judgments are inconsistent.

AHP theory is also tied in to ongoing research in the related field of asset investing. An evaluation of recent research shows that it has solid and effective consistent measurements. The strength of Sedzro et al.'s (2012) theory is that it clearly defines how the theory attempts to eliminate bias judgment. This article discussed AHP from a general point of view, in comparison to other recent articles that described AHP in more specific terms.

Pair Wise Comparisons

According to Vaidya and Kumar (2006), AHP theory synthesizes and prioritizes the differences between factors. AHP theory integrates a pair wise comparison approach to decision making. An ordinal sequence of variables is developed from top priority to bottom priority. This is an Eigen value approach to the pair-wise comparisons (Vaidya & Kumar, 2006). After a thorough review of the literature and this seminal article, it explains that AHP provides a method for quantifying decisions for the decision maker.

According to AHP literature, quantitative and qualitative values are methodically rated on a numeric scale. An understanding of and the ability to employ the AHP includes understanding the 1 to 9 criteria scale that AHP uses. The Vaidya and Kumar (2006) article described some of the AHP component in contrast to AHP theories, as seen in the other articles.

Vaidya and Kumar (2006) outlined the steps necessary to employ the AHP theory. Some key and basic steps involved in this methodology are

1. State the problem.

2. Broaden the objectives of the problem or consider all actors, objectives and its outcome.

3. Identify the criteria that influence the behavior

4. Structure the problem in a hierarchy of different levels constituting goal, criteria, sub-criteria and alternatives (Vaidya & Kumar).

AHP helps to incorporate a group consensus. Generally, this consists of a questionnaire for comparison of each element and geometric mean to arrive at a final solution (Vaidya & Kumar, 2006). End results are determined by measuring and comparing the values of individual factors. AHP theory and research is applicable and relevant to the decision-making process.

Decision-Making Process

The scholarly article by Al-Harbi (2001) focused on the quantitative integration of alternatives into the decision making process. This recent article reveals the strengths of synthesizing both AHP's quantitative and qualitative properties. The opinion of the decision-maker is used to numerically prioritize a number of differing elements. A thorough review of the literature shows that AHP is a step-by-step systematic process. Al-Harbi posited the strength of this approach is that it organizes tangible and intangible factors in a systematic way.

According to AHP literature, AHP adds structure and simplicity to the decision making process. The Al-Harbi (2001) article discusses the common problems that AHP is designed to solve and a means of employing this research methods. The other articles do not focus on the type of problems that this theory could solve. By breaking down large problems into smaller logical pieces, one is able to connect, through simple paired comparison judgments, the small to the large (Al-Harbi, 2001). The strength of this recent article is that it shows the complexity of problems that the AHP process can solve. Problems faced by project managers are becoming increasingly difficult.

The Al-Harbi (2001) article explained that the AHP theory and research is applicable to multiple decision-making criteria. The elements of the problems are numerous, and the interrelationships among the elements are extremely complicated. It is difficult to understand how a large number of different elements relate to each other. The article provides a brief overview of decision theory and also provides a logical connection between AHP and decision theory.

Relationships between elements of a problem may be highly nonlinear (Al-Harbi, 2001). A number of similar elements sometimes have different weights and values. This recent article integrates AHP scholarly research with today's complex but practical problem solving. A thorough review of the literature reveals that AHP theory is designed to give decision makers a better understanding of their problems. Finally, Al-Harbi explained how AHP synthesizes a set of problems using a set of alternatives.

AHP Strengths and Weaknesses

Cheng, Li, and Ho (2002) explained some of AHP's strengths and weaknesses. The article provided evidence showing that although analytic hierarchy process is effective to use for management decision making, it can be defective if used improperly. AHP becomes one of the essential multi-criteria, decision-making methods used by both management practitioners and academics (Cheng et al., 2002).

Cheng et al. (2002) posited that AHP has become firmly integrated in the multi-criteria decision-making process. The role of AHP theory in the current decision-making discipline is carefully outlined in this article. The current role of AHP is outlined less in the other articles. With the development of computer software packages, its usage expands vastly across different business and management areas.

This quantitative research study explained how technology has helped to enable the use of AHP theory. AHP is a kind of multiple criteria decision making (Cheng et al., 2002). This recent research explains the origin of AHP and some of the factors that motivated Saaty to develop the process. Saaty (1980) developed AHP in the early 1970s in response to the scarce resources allocation and planning needs for the military.

The strength of this recent article is that it explains a purpose that one might use to carry out the AHP process. It helps to decompose an unstructured problem into a rational decision hierarchy, similar to a decision tree (Cheng et al., 2002). In summary, this article discussed how problems are decomposed using AHP theory similar to regression analysis.

A synthesis of relevant AHP theory and research described how the theory organizes decision hierarchy in a fashion similar to a tree. It can elicit more information   from the experts or decision-makers by employing the pair-wise comparison of individual groups of elements (Cheng et al., 2002). According to relevant theory and research in this article, pair-wise companions are integrated to create the hierarchy.

The Cheng et al. (2002) article went on to explain how relevant weighted elements are to AHP theory and research synthesis pair-wise comparisons. The article's strength is that it combined both quantitative and qualitative elements of AHP theory. It used the consistency measure to validate the consistency of the rating from the experts and decision-makers (Cheng et al., 2002). Cheng et al. focused on the mixed nature of AHP research, more so than do the other research articles reviewed. The AHP theory integrates quantitative and qualitative elements in its approach. It is, therefore, argued to be composed of both qualitative and quantitative substances.

A subset of both recent and seminal articles incorporates the mixed nature of AHP research. Mixing both elements strengthens AHP research by adding diversity and triangulation. It can help to prioritize (rank) elements in order to identify the key elements (Cheng et al., 2002). Through prioritization, the AHP theory synthesizes key elements according to this recent article.

The Cheng et al. (2002) article points out the need to rate elements of a problem in greater detail than other recent articles. The strength of this research is that it describes the importance of elemental hierarchy in the decision-making process. When an organization works on several projects simultaneously, ranking the relative importance level of individual tasks may help better allocate the resources. Finally, this recent article outlines the important role that AHP can play in an organization's decision making process.

Synthesis of AHP Literature

Many outstanding works have been published based on AHP. They include applications from a number of different fields of studies. The field of study of strategic planning has been influenced by AHP. This recent article shows AHP's versatility as compared to the other article, which discussed the technical aspects of AHP.

Projects often succeed based on the reliability of its decision-making. The design problem is concerned with the identification of a preferred alternative from a potentially infinite set of alternatives implicitly defined by a set of constraints (Al-Harbi, 2001). A number of limited alternatives often form the core of problem statements. The Al-Harbi (2001) article focused more on the practical aspect of making complex decisions as compared to the other articles. This recent article establishes a more systematic approach to viewing problem solving and decision making, as compared to the other articles. Saaty's (1994) article described how the theory can be used in greater detail than the other articles reviewed in the literature.

AHP can be applied to any allocation of resources and choice prediction problems (Wind & Saaty, 1980). Though it is not the focus of the article, the article does integrate and synthesize relevant theory and research with practical application of the theory. The Saaty (1994) article does integrate more theory and application as compared to the other seminal article. The AHP focuses on dominance matrices and their corresponding measurement (Wind & Saaty, 1980). This seminal research focuses on hierarchy based on the results of instrumental measurements. Dominance and measurements are the focus of this article.

Data from Canadian mutual funds over a total period of five years and three months illustrated theories of dominance and measurement (Sedzro et al., 2012). AHP analysis is used to study problems over the long term. A recent longitudinal study described the integration of AHP in the practical discipline of investing. Sedzro et al. outlined recent data of AHP used for investments. As a comparison, longitudinal results were released in this article and were not in the other articles.

In contrast to the other AHP articles, the Sedzro et al. (2012) article described how the theory organizes components according to a hierarchy in order to incorporate significant quantities of information. The article paints a comprehensive view of problem solving. According to the Sedzro et al. article, priorities are set by pair-wise comparisons and by assigning weights to different criteria. In comparison to the other articles, Cheng's et al. (2002) article explained the usefulness of pair–wise comparisons. It sets the computations to assign weights to the elements.

Conclusion

In conclusion, this literature review summarized a subset of both recent and seminal peer-reviewed journal articles which deal in some way with analytical hierarchy process (AHP) theory. The literature review went further to compare and contrasts three of the articles from that subset. This review identified and explained the strengths and weaknesses of each of the three articles. A summary of both the recent and seminal articles revealed that the more recent articles deal with practical research, while the seminal articles addressed general AHP theory (Wind & Saaty, 1980). The relevant empirical theory and research of these articles is based on comparative measurements. According to Wind and Saaty, the basic premise of the analytic hierarchy process is that measurement evolves out of comparisons, particularly pairwise comparisons.

CHAPTER 3. METHODOLOGY

Introduction

Quantitative research lends itself to IT security studies that deal with mobile computing devices because IT security needs to provide precise solutions to counter threats against these devices. The current study employed a probabilistic model that analyzed and provided findings on the impact of (CEMD) certified e-mail message delivery (Basagiannis et al., 2011). Using the analytical hierarchy process (AHP) methodology, a list of five information security elements was identified and their relative importance was evaluated. Evaluating the defense in-depth strategy in terms of current threats provides additional insight into the key aspects of the strategy (Cleghorn, 2013).

According to Vaidya and Kumar (2006), AHP is a multiple criteria decision-making tool. AHP theory synthesizes and prioritizes the differences between factors and integrates a pair-wise comparison approach to decision making (Vaidya & Kumar, 2006). An ordinal sequence of variables was developed from top prior to bottom priority; a quantitative research method was chosen because of the nature of this research.

Creswell (2009) explained that the selection of a research design is also based on the nature of the research problem or issue being addressed, as well as the researcher's personal experiences, and the audiences of the study. Study participants for this dissertation research were emailed a survey requesting that they prioritize five defense in-depth information assurance measures–anti-virus; intrusion detection; password; smart-cards; and encryption, ranging from (1-5) using a Likert scale. The prioritization was based on standard cost, effectiveness, and perceived ease of use in terms of protecting organizational computing devices.

The measures were then weighted, based on ranking. A pair-wise comparison of each of the five measures was then made using the analytical hierarchy model to determine whether the Likert scale and the AHP model could be effectively applied to the prioritization of information assurance measures to protect organizational computing devices. The pair-wise comparison was designed to connect the larger problem of protecting organizational computing devices with the smaller problem of prioritizing defense in-depth measures.

According to Al-Harbi (2001), by breaking a problem down in a logical fashion from the large to the smallest, one is able to connect, through simple paired comparison judgments, the large to the small. The comparison algorithm began with a set of pair-wise comparison matrices (size $n \times n$) for each of the measures, with one matrix for each measure. The pair-wise comparisons were done in terms of which element dominated the other (Al-Harbi, 2001).

If the AHP model cannot be effectively applied, then information technology analysts must rely on alternative decision-making models to determine the prioritization of defense in-depth measures. Is this a one-time solves all or is it a process that must be repeated for each unique organization based on their unique mission and circumstances? This is a process that must be repeated for each unique organization based on its unique mission and circumstances.

Research Question

What is the relationship between an information technology analyst's prioritization of defense in-depth measures and the effectiveness in protecting organizational devices against cyber-attacks? Answering the research question provides value to the scholarly and practitioner information assurance communities by providing additional methods for defeating cyber-attacks.

Hypothesis

H_0 Null Hypothesis. AHP does not affect the relationship between the information technology analyst's prioritization of five defense in-depth dependent variables–anti-virus; firewalls; intrusion detection systems; passwords; and encryptions–and the independent variables of cost, ease of use, and effectiveness in protecting organizational devices against cyber-attacks.

H_1 AHP does affect the relationship between the information technology analyst's prioritization of five defense in-depth information assurance measures (dependent variables)–anti-virus; firewalls; intrusion detection systems; passwords; and encryptions–and the independent variables of standard cost, perceived ease of use, and effectiveness in protecting organizational devices against cyber-attacks.

Research Sub question

R1. How should information assurance information technology analysts prioritize five information assurance defense in-depth measures–firewalls; intrusion detection systems; anti-virus; passwords; and smartcards–to protect their organization's mobile computing devices against cyber-attacks keeping in mind standard cost, perceived ease of use, and effectiveness?

Investigative Questions

1. Of the five most common information assurance measures (firewalls, intrusion detection systems, passwords, and smartcards), rank them in terms of cost of implementing: $1 = least\ costly$ and $5 = most\ costly$.

2. Of the five most common information assurance measures (firewalls, intrusion detection systems, anti-virus, passwords, and smartcards), rank them in terms of maintenance cost: $1 = least\ costly$ and $5 = most\ costly$.

3. Of the five most common information assurance measures (firewalls, intrusion detection systems, anti-virus, passwords, and smartcards), rank them in terms of life-cycle cost: 1 = *least costly* and 5 = *most costly*.

4. Of the five most common information assurance measures (firewalls, intrusion detection systems, anti-virus, passwords, and smartcards), rank them in terms of ease of use for employees: 1 = *easiest* and 5 = *most difficult*.

5. Of the five most common information assurance measures (firewalls, intrusion detection systems, passwords, and smartcards), rank them in terms of ease of use for technicians: 1 = *easiest to use* and 5 = *most difficult*.

6. Of the five most common information assurance measures (firewalls, intrusion detection systems, passwords, and smartcards), rank them in terms of effectively stopping viruses: 1 = *most effective* and 5 = *least effective*.

7. Of the five most common information assurance measures (firewalls, intrusion detection systems, anti-virus, passwords, and smartcards), rank them in terms of effectiveness in stopping hacking: 1 = *most effective* and 5 being the least effective.

8. Of the five most common information assurance measures (firewalls, intrusion detection systems, passwords, and smartcards), rank them in terms of ease of use for management: 1 = *easiest to use* and 5 = *most difficult*.

9. Of the five most common information assurance measures (firewalls, intrusion detection systems, anti-virus, passwords, and smartcards), rank them in terms of effectiveness in stopping hacking: 1 = *most effective* and 5 = *least effective*.

Research Design

This non-experimental survey research design was used to survey a simple random sample frame of 954 active Survey Monkey registered information technology analysts. A link to the survey was emailed to Survey Monkey registered information technology analysts, asking them to prioritize five defense in-depth measures based on standard cost, perceived ease of use, and effectiveness. The prioritization was done using a Likert scale instrument with a (1-5) prioritization of the five measures.

Population

As of May 2013, there were 78,020 information technology analysts in the United States (Bureau of Labor Statistics, 2015). The information technology analysts who were chosen for this study had one to 20 years of experience working with defense in-depth information assurance measures with their employers. The employees ranged from entry level employees to supervisors and managers.

Sample

The sample frame consisted of 954 currently employed active Survey Monkey registered information technology analysts from the population of 78,020. There were a total of 100 responses from the sample frame of 954 Survey Monkey registered information technology analysts. The sample size was calculated using a Gpower3 (Faul, Erdfelder, Buchner, & Lang, 2009) calculation (Figure 2).

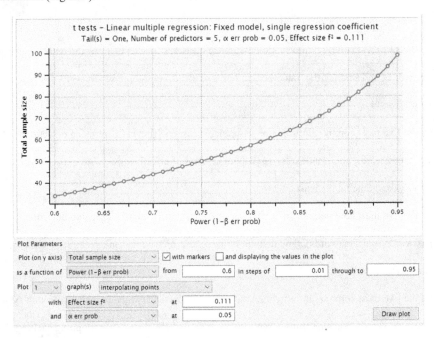

Figure 2. Sample size calculated by the Gpower3 model.

Sampling Procedure

The 954 potential participants were required to be registered with Survey Monkey. A survey was e-mailed to the analysts asking them to prioritize five defense in-depth measures based on standard cost, perceived ease of use, and prevention ability. Having a random sample with known probabilities of selection enables the researcher to estimate the sampling error (Lavrakas, 2008). That is, the researcher can use the sample to make inferences for the target population and to estimate the precision of the sample-based estimates.

The randomization process, defined by SurveyMonkey.com consists of a program that takes the nth record from the database of ~954, based on the quantity of survey responses ordered. For this research, the program used the total number of information technology analysts, and given the order size of 100, selected the first record in the 954 set, the

501, the 401, and so on, until 100 surveys were selected. Although this process did not meet the strict definition of statistical randomization, it provided a simple randomized sample of surveys from the database of 954, which was acceptable for this research.

Sample Size

Statistical power 1-β is computed as a function of significance level α, sample size, and population effect size (Faul et al., 2009). Sampling used Gpower3 to determine a sample size large enough to develop external validity and so that the result might be generalized to the entire population of 78,020 information technology analysts working in the United States (Faul et al., 2009). Cronbach's Alpha .80 or above was also used to determine reliability. Given a sample frame size of 954 information technology analysts, with a margin of error of 5% and a confidence level of 95%, a simple random sample size of 954 was calculated. Given 954 Survey Monkey surveys, and the anticipated response rate of 11%, the anticipated number of samples collected was calculated to be 100 (954 x .11; Faul et al., 2009). If the recruitment process had resulted in fewer than the 100 samples required by Gpower3, the fallback procedure was to expand the sample frame to additional information security professional groups listed on Survey Monkey (e.g., the Information Security Career Professionals Group).

Instrumentation

The web-based survey provided by the online survey provider Survey Monkey included functionality to allow definition and implementation of web pages that included logic to ensure the completion of the data entry of the pages and to manage the four pages as a complete unit of work for the survey. The software managing the survey controlled both the data entry selections available to the participants and the start-to-finish completion of the entire survey. Therefore, the survey design ensured participants completed the survey based on the software parameters that were configured for the pages before they were allowed survey submission. The prioritization was conducted using the Likert Scale Instrument with a (1-5) prioritization of the five measures.

Data Collection

A simple random sample of 100 information technology analysts from a population of 78,020 information technology analysts in the United States were e-mailed a survey, asking them to prioritize five defense in-depth measures based on cost, ease of use, and prevention ability. Sampling used Gpower3 to determine a sample size large enough to develop external validity and so that results can be generalized to the entire population of 78,020 information technology analysts (Faul et al., 2009). Cronbach's Alpha .80 or above was also used to determine validity.

Informed consent was obtained at the end of the survey. Data will be held for seven years and then destroyed. There was no conflict of interest because the researcher had no affiliation with the participants. The surveys were collected anonymously and all privately identifying information, including participant IP addresses, was not collected.

Data Analysis

The data analysis was conducted using a Likert Scale, with a (1-5) prioritization of the five defense in-depth measures and the AHP model to conduct a pair-wise comparison of each of the five measures. The research methods used in the study provided the advantage of using statistics to make inferences about larger groups, using very small samples, referred to as generalizability (Cooper & Schindler, 2008). The findings are presented in the results section.

Correlation Methodology

Information Technology Analysts Survey Procedures

1. Send the survey to 954 Survey Monkey Information technology analysts.

2. Randomly select the sample from the population of returned surveys.

3. Code and analyze data (responses) from the sample using an SPSS tool.

4. Code and analyze data (responses) from the sample using the AHP procedure.

Analytical Hierarchy Process Procedures

1. Define the problem and determine its goal.

2. Structure the hierarchy from the top (the objectives from a decision-maker's viewpoint) through the intermediate levels (criteria on which subsequent levels depend) to the lowest level which usually contains the list of alternatives.

3. Construct a set of pair-wise comparison matrices (size n x n) for each of the lower levels, with one matrix for each element in the level immediately above by using the relative scale measurement. The pair-wise comparisons were done in terms of which element dominates the other.

4. There were $n(n-1)/$ judgments required to develop the set of matrices in Step 3. Reciprocals were automatically assigned in each pair-wise comparison.

5. Hierarchical synthesis was then used to weight the eigenvectors by the weights of the criteria, and the sum was taken over all weighted eigenvector entries corresponding to those in the next lower level of the hierarchy.

6. Having made all the pair-wise comparisons, the consistency was determined by using the eigenvalue, max, to calculate the consistency index, CI as follows: CI (max . $- n$) / ($n - 1$), where n is the matrix size. Judgment consistency was checked by taking the consistency ratio (CR) of CI with the appropriate value. The CR was acceptable, since it did not exceed 0.10. If it had been more, the judgment matrix would have been inconsistent. To obtain a consistent matrix, judgments should be reviewed and improved.

7. Steps 3 through 6 were performed for all levels in the hierarchy (Al-Harbi, 2001).

Validity and Reliability

Validity and reliability are important concepts in developing and implementing research in a correlational study. Researchers view reliability as the conceptual repeatability of the experiment with the same results (Cooper & Schindler, 2008). Holton and Burnett (2005) considered measure data valid when they quantified what was to be measured; this often includes determinations of both accuracy and precision.

Another characterization often expressed with reliability is internal consistency, a standard by which researchers feel they can rely on the reported research measurements, determinations, and conclusions (Cooper & Schindler, 2008). The research methods used in the study provided the advantage of using statistics to make inferences about larger groups using very small samples, referred to as generalizability (Cooper & Schindler, 2008). This ability to apply the external validity or the transferability of the findings concept of generalizability also establishes trustworthiness in data analysis of quantitative research (Cooper & Schindler, 2008).

Validity of new measures was confirmed with both convergent and discriminate validity testing of the construct; criterion-related validity further reinforced the precision and accuracy beliefs of the measured values (Hinkin, 2005). The research analyses were applied to these methodologies in the data analysis to add to the rigor and robustness of the constructs' validity. An interim correlation analysis was first performed on the variables, and any variables less than .4, and all other variables were deleted (Hinkin, 2005).

A preliminary factor analysis using the principal components analysis method; item loadings examinations using the Kaiser criterion; and a screen test of analysis of variance of the deductive approach supported theoretical distinctions of the measures developed in the research (Hinkin, 2005). According to Straub, Boudreau, and Gefen (2004), the research analyses applied the validity guidelines and also included an assessment of the study's internal consistency by calculating internal consistencies for each new construct using statistical tests (Passmore & Baker, 2005).

In addition, for reliability, the research statistical analyses interpreted effect sizes and variables of the factor analysis, particularly by ensuring the independence variables of the factor analysis (Yang, 2005). These statistical approaches to testing the validity and reliability were also complemented by the field test conducted, which bolstered the study's constructs and measurements in the pursuit of validity and reliability (Cooper & Schindler, 2008).

Ethical Considerations

The potential benefits of research in organizations, especially public safety organizations, can be very beneficial, but there are risks that some employees or the organization could be unfairly stigmatized. This study was conducted with the informed consent of all of the participants. The participants were not subjected to risk. To avoid conflict of interest, the survey participants are in no way related to the researcher.

This research study addressed ethical considerations in three areas. First, the research required human participants and, therefore, the research design methodology required approval of an Institutional Review Board (IRB) in order to conduct the study. The research design methodology requested and received approval from the Capella University's IRB for research of human subjects.

The research design methodology addressed the considerations for privacy, anonymity, confidentiality, respect for persons, beneficence, and justice for the study participants (U.S. Department of Health and Human Services [U.S. DHHS], 1979). Rights to privacy, anonymity, and confidentiality of the study included the protection of study participants by creating a research process that ensured their anonymity. The design included the protection of the actual identity of all participants (anonymity); the subjects' e-mail addresses provided in their magazine subscription application was used only to communicate the Internet web address link (URL) to the online survey.

The research design provided very strict efforts to ensure anonymity and confidentiality of research participants and provided reasonable protection of privacy rights. These last three research ethics topics in this area, respect for persons, beneficence, and justice for the study participants, have foundational representation in the *Belmont Report* (U.S. DHHS, 1979), which states that basic ethical principles and guidelines are to be used to resolve the ethical problems for the conduct of research with human subjects. The *Belmont Report* identifies three basic ethical principles for conducting research with human subjects: respect for persons, beneficence, and justice (U.S. DHHS, 1979).

In this research study, the design addressed the respect for persons' principles by treating individuals (human participants) as autonomous agents, capable of making decisions and choices, and recognizing and planning for the special protection for any persons with diminished autonomy (Bryant, 2005). For specifically addressing autonomous agency, the design included an informed consent process to ensure that participation was voluntary, with adequate information provided to participants to make their decision of whether or not to participate (U.S. DHHS, 1979). Specifically addressing diminished autonomy, while ensuring extra protection is afforded to prevent harm from exclusion, the design

39

used a web-based online survey methodology with potential participants included from a compiled database of IT security professionals.

This reasonably ensured that potential subjects in the database had contractually agreed to the terms of the information security magazine subscription, which was used by the vendor list to compile the list. In this research study, the design addressed the obligation to protection of human subjects (beneficence) guidelines and principles by including considerations for the individual subject of the study, and the larger society's benefits of the study (U.S. DHHS, 1979). In this risk and benefit analysis for subjects and the larger societal interests, the research planning and resulting design were considered to present no risk to either.

It was determined that the negative risks to would not change whether or not the research was conducted. The research planning and evaluation determined that those participating would benefit indirectly by helping to advance the knowledge and understanding of the professional field, and potentially benefit directly by the gained satisfaction that they contributed to the advancement of knowledge and understanding in their professional field. This positive result may also include the satisfaction that they potentially contributed to the future direction and influenced the field of study. This is further supported in the study by informing the participants that they can obtain access to the tabulated summarized results of the survey in which they participated in the final published dissertation.

In this research study, the design addressed the obligation to equality in the burden of human subject research (justice) guidelines and principles by including considerations for equal and fair distribution of any burden created by the study (U.S. DHHS, 1979). In particular, the ethical justice analyses for this research determined that no perceived or imparted burden would result from the study. Again, the effects or impacts on participants of the study are determined not to have been different if the research had not been conducted. Moreover, given that participation was voluntary and withdraws from the study was available at any time, the guidelines and principles for justice were reasonably addressed for the study.

The final area of consideration for ethics of the research included the disclosure of areas of limitations or concerns, and suggestions for future research (Cooper & Schindler, 2008). The limitations or concerns that often stem from specific areas of research methodology were previously addressed; this explanation is provided to address the ethical importance in disclosing areas where previous research has determined such limitations (Cooper & Schindler, 2008).

In this research, the researcher acknowledges limitations related to the use of online survey data collection and correlational research (Cooper & Schindler, 2008). The limitations or concerns can also stem from weaknesses or issues detected by the researcher in conducting the study, such as implementations issues (Cooper & Schindler, 2008). For the other consideration of research ethics, the research design addressed the suggestions for further investigations. The topic often relates to the acknowledged limitations and suggests methodologies or practices to address the limitations (Cooper & Schindler, 2008). For example, in a study where the research design used a small sample size, researchers may recommend a larger sample to add to the rigor and strength of the research (Cooper & Schindler, 2008). For this research, a further research recommendations section is provided after the limitations section for the accumulated recommendations.

CHAPTER 4. RESULTS

Introduction

Chapter 4 consists of a description the population and sample. The purpose of this chapter is to present the analysis which rejects the H_0 null hypothesis that AHP does not affect the relationship between the information technology analysts' prioritization of five defense in-depth dependent variables (anti-virus; firewalls; intrusion detection systems; passwords; and encryptions) and the independent variables of cost, ease of use, and effectiveness in protecting organizational devices against cyber-attacks. The data capture (recording) and coding methodology employed in this study was used to determine the best defense in-depth choices from a list of decision alternatives. Finally, a summary of the results are included in this chapter.

The study started with an electronic mail to 954 randomly sampled prospective participants. The respondents included three categories: (a) those that clicked the link in the e-mail but did not complete the survey, (b) those who did not agree to participant in the study, and (c) those that completed the survey and agreed to participate in the study. The breakdown response rate for the study was: 177 responded by clicking the survey link, 120 agreed to participate, and 100 completed the survey.

Collection and Missing Data Analysis

The data collected were reviewed for missing values. The only missing values occurred for checklist variables which were expected by design, or where the participant discontinued the survey entry. All other variables were populated as expected, or if missing, were not entered. The first data variable collected in the survey was the "agree to participate" question, the informed consent. The only surveys included in the data downloaded from the collectors were those in which the participants agreed to participate.

Description of Population

The demographics of the surveys used reflects demographics that are consistent with U.S.-based IT professionals from an approximate 78,020 active U.S. information technology analysts population sample contained in the Survey Monkey database that was used to initially contact the potential participants via e-mail. The graphics in Figures 2 and 3 represent the gender and age charts for the sampled participants.

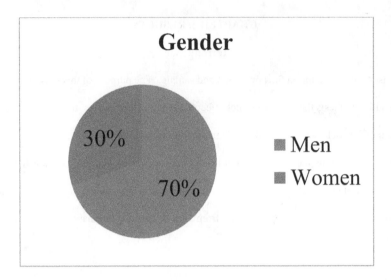

Figure 3. Gender of Sample

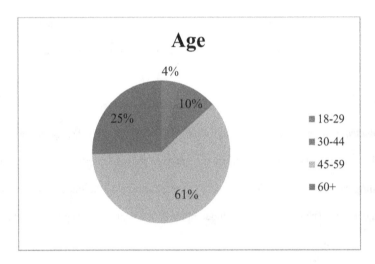

Figure 4. Ages of Sample

Investigative Questions

The study design included nine investigative questions which provided foundation for the main research questions. This section lists each investigative question and includes the statistical analysis to explore each sub question.

Investigative Question 1

43

Of the five most common information assurance measures (firewalls, intrusion detection systems, passwords, and smartcards); rank them in terms of cost of implementation with 1 being the least costly and 5 being the most costly. A pair-wise comparison is shown in Table 1, and a hierarchical synthesis used to weight the eigenvectors is shown in Table 2.

Table 1
Implementation Cost Pair-Wise Comparison

Pair-wise Comparison	Implementation Cost				

Standardized Matrix	Implementation Cost				
	Passwords	Antivirus	Firewalls	Smartcards	IDS	W-Vector (Weight)
A. Passwords (3.76)	0.31	0.25	0.25	0.25	0.25	26.20%
B. Antivirus (3.10)	0.25	0.21	0.21	0.21	0.21	21.60%
C. Firewalls (3.00)	0.25	0.20	0.20	0.20	0.20	20.90%
D. Smartcards (2.65)	0.22	0.18	0.18	0.18	0.18	18.46%
E. IDS (2.49)	0.20	0.17	0.17	0.17	0.17	17.35%
Sum	1.2254902	1	1	1	1	

	Passwords	Antivirus	Firewalls	Smartcards	IDS
A. Passwords (3.76)	1.00	1.21	1.25	1.42	1.51
B. Antivirus (3.10)	3.10	1.00	1.03	1.17	1.24
C. Firewalls (3.00)	3.00	0.97	1.00	1.13	1.20
D. Smartcards (2.65)	2.65	0.85	0.88	1.00	1.06
E. IDS (2.49)	2.49	0.80	0.83	0.94	1.00
Sum	12.24	4.84	5.00	5.66	6.02

Table 2
Implementation Cost Standardized Matrix

The consistency index (CI) (Λ max - n)/(n - 1), gives information about logical consistency among pair-wise comparison judgments in a perfect pair-wise comparison case. When CI = 0.0, there is no logical inconsistency among the pair-wise comparison judgments, or the judgment is considered 100% consistent (Utugizaki et al., 2007). The consistency ratio (CR) is a measure of how consistent the judgments have been relative to large samples of purely random judgements. If the CR is much in excess of 0.1, the judgments are untrustworthy (Geoff, 2004).

In Table 3, the consistency ratio is provided. The consistency ratio of 0.01 shows that the pair-wise comparison does not exceed 0.10 and is considered acceptable. The results of the information technology analyst survey and the AHP consistency index table (Table 3) show that passwords have moderately (6.55) less implementation cost than the other four information assurance measures.

Investigative Question 2

Of the five most common information assurance measures (firewalls, intrusion detection systems, anti-virus, passwords, and smartcards), rank them in terms of maintenance cost with: 1 = *least costly* and 5 = *most costly*. In Table 4, the consistency ratio is provided. The consistency ratio of 0.01 shows that the pair-wise comparison does not exceed 0.10

and is considered acceptable. The results of the information technology analyst survey and the AHP consistency index table (Table 4) show that passwords also have moderately (6.38) less maintenance costs than the other four information assurance measures.

Investigative Question 3

Of the five most common information assurance measures (firewalls, intrusion detection systems, anti-virus, passwords, and smartcards), rank them in terms of life-cycle cost with: 1 = *least costly* and 5 = *most costly*. In Table 5, the consistency ratio is provided. The consistency ratio of 0.01 shows that the pair-wise comparison does not exceed 0.10 and is considered acceptable. The results of the information technology analyst survey and the AHP consistency index table (Table 5) show that passwords have moderately (6.55) less life-cycle costs than the other four information assurance measures.

Table 3
Implementation Cost Consistency Index

Consistency Index	Implementation Cost						
	Passwords	Antivirus	Firewalls	Smartcards	IDS	Sum	W-Vector (Weight)
A. Passwords (3.76)	0.31	0.25	0.25	0.25	0.25	1.31	6.55
B. Antivirus (3.10)	0.25	0.21	0.21	0.21	0.21	1.08	5.40
C. Firewalls (3.00)	0.25	0.20	0.20	0.20	0.20	1.05	5.23
D. Smartcards (2.65)	0.22	0.18	0.18	0.18	0.18	0.92	4.62
E. IDS (2.49)	0.20	0.17	0.17	0.17	0.17	0.87	4.34
					Lambda		5.23
				Consistency Index	CI		0.05
				Consistency Ratio	CR		0.01

Note. $p = cr < 0.10$.

Table 4

Consistency Index		Maintenance Cost					
	Firewalls	IDS	Passwords	Antivirus	Smartcards	Sum	W-Vector (Weight)
A. Passwords (3.67)	0.30	0.24	0.24	0.24	0.24	1.28	6.38
B. Firewalls (3.16)	0.26	0.21	0.21	0.21	0.21	1.10	5.49
C. Anti-virus (2.84)	0.23	0.19	0.19	0.19	0.19	0.99	4.93
D. IDS (2.70)	0.22	0.18	0.18	0.18	0.18	0.94	4.69
E. Smartcards (2.64)	0.21	0.18	0.18	0.18	0.18	0.92	4.59
						Lambda	5.22
				Consistency Index	CI	0.05	
				Consistency Ratio	CR	0.01	

Maintenance Cost Consistency Index

Note. $p = cr < 0.10$.

Investigative Question 4

Of the five most common information assurance measures (firewalls, intrusion detection systems, anti-virus, passwords, and smartcards), rank them in terms of ease of use for employees with: 1 = *easiest* and 5 = *most difficult*. In Table 6, the consistency ratio is provided. The consistency ratio of 0.01 shows that the pair-wise comparison does not exceed the level of 0.10 and is considered acceptable. The results of the information technology analyst survey and the AHP consistency index table (Table 6) show that firewalls are slightly (5.70) easier for employees to use in comparison to the other four information assurance measures.

Investigative Question 5

Of the five most common information assurance measures (firewalls, intrusion detection systems, passwords, and smartcards), rank them in terms of ease of use for technicians with: 1 = *easiest to use* and 5 = *most difficult*. In Table 7, the consistency ratio is provided. The consistency ratio of 0.01 shows that the pair-wise comparison does not exceed 0.10 and is considered acceptable. The results of the Information technology analyst survey and the AHP consistency index table (Table 7) show that passwords are moderately (6.79) easier for technicians to use, in comparison to the other four information assurance measures.

Table 5
Life-Cycle Cost Consistency Index

Consistency Index	Life-Cycle Cost						
	Passwords	Firewalls	Antivirus	IDS	Smartcards	sum	W-Vector (Weight)
A. Passwords (3.66)	0.30	0.24	0.24	0.24	0.24	1.27	6.36
B. Firewalls (3.15)	0.26	0.21	0.21	0.21	0.21	1.10	5.48
C. Antivirus (2.93)	0.24	0.20	0.20	0.20	0.20	1.02	5.09
D. IDS (2.72)	0.22	0.18	0.18	0.18	0.18	0.95	4.73
E. Smartcards (2.54)	0.21	0.17	0.17	0.17	0.17	0.88	4.42
						Lambda	5.22
					Consistency Index	CI	0.05
					Consistency Ratio	CR	0.01

Note. $p = $ cr < 0.10.

Table 6

Consistency Index	Ease of Use Employees						
	Firewalls	Passwords	Antivirus	Smartcards	IDS	sum	W-Vector (Weight)
A. Firewalls (3.30)	0.26	0.22	0.22	0.22	0.22	1.14	5.70
B. Passwords (3.23)	0.25	0.22	0.22	0.22	0.22	1.12	5.58
C. Antivirus (3.17)	0.25	0.21	0.21	0.21	0.21	1.09	5.47
D. Smartcards (2.77)	0.22	0.18	0.18	0.18	0.18	0.96	4.78
E. IDS (2.53)	0.20	0.17	0.17	0.17	0.17	0.87	4.37
						Lambda	5.18
					Consistency Index	CI	0.05
					Consistency Ratio	CR	0.01

Employees' Ease of Use Consistency Index

Note. $p = $ cr < 0.10.

nvestigative Question 6

Of the five most common information assurance measures (firewalls, intrusion detection systems, passwords, and smartcards), rank them in terms of ease of use for management with: 1 = *easiest to use* and 5 = *most difficult*. In Table 8, the consistency ratio is provided. The consistency ratio of 0.01 shows that the pair-wise comparison does not exceed 0.10 and is considered acceptable. The results of the information technology analyst survey and the AHP consistency index table (Table 8) show that passwords are moderately (6.26) easier for management to use, in comparison to the other four information assurance measures.

Investigative Question 7

Of the five most common information assurance measures (firewalls, intrusion detection systems, passwords, and smartcards), rank them in terms of effectively stopping viruses with: 1 = *most effective* and 5 = *least effective*. In Table 9, the consistency ratio is provided. The consistency ratio of 0.01 shows that the pair-wise comparison does not exceed 0.10 and is considered acceptable. The results of the information technology analyst survey and the AHP consistency index table (Table 9) show that firewalls are significantly (7.22) more effective at stopping viruses, in comparison to the other four information assurance measures.

Table 7

Consistency Index	Ease of Use Technicians						
	Passwords	Antivirus	Firewalls	Smartcards	IDS	Sum	W-Vector (Weight)
A. Passwords (3.89)	0.32	0.26	0.26	0.26	0.26	1.36	6.79
B. Antivirus (3.13)	0.26	0.21	0.21	0.21	0.21	1.09	5.47
C. Firewalls (2.99)	0.25	0.20	0.20	0.20	0.20	1.04	5.22
D. Smartcards (2.87)	0.24	0.19	0.19	0.19	0.19	1.00	5.01
E. IDS (2.12)	0.18	0.14	0.14	0.14	0.14	0.74	3.70
						Lambda	5.24
					Consistency Index	CI	0.05
					Consistency Ratio	CR	0.01

Technicians' Ease of Use Consistency Index

Note. $p = cr < 0.10$.

Table 8

Consistency Index	Ease of Use Management						
	Password	Firewalls	Antivirus	Smartcards	IDS	Sum	W-Vector (Weight)
A. Passwords (3.60)	0.29	0.24	0.24	0.24	0.24	1.25	6.26
B. Firewalls (3.09)	0.25	0.21	0.21	0.21	0.21	1.07	5.37
C. Antivirus (3.03)	0.24	0.20	0.20	0.20	0.20	1.05	5.27
D. Smartcards (2.84)	0.23	0.19	0.19	0.19	0.19	0.99	4.94
E. IDS (2.43)	0.20	0.16	0.16	0.16	0.16	0.84	4.22
						Lambda	5.21
					Consistency Ratio	CR	0.05
					Consistency Ratio	CR	0.01

Management's Ease of Use Consistency Index

Note. $p = cr < 0.10$.

Investigative Question 8

Of the five most common information assurance measures (firewalls, intrusion detection systems, anti-virus, passwords, and smartcards), rank them in terms of effectiveness in stopping hacking with: 1 = *most effective* and 5 = *least effective*. In Table 10 the consistency ratio is provided. The consistency ratio of 0.01 shows that the pair-wise comparison does not exceed 0.10 and is considered acceptable. The results of the information technology analysts survey and the AHP consistency index table (Table 10) show that firewalls are significantly (7.32) more effective at stopping hacking, in comparison to the other four information assurance measures.

Investigative Question 9

Of the five most common information assurance measures (firewalls, intrusion detection systems, anti-virus, passwords, and smartcards), rank them in terms of effectiveness in stopping denial of service (DoS) attacks, with 1 being the most effective and 5 being the least effective. In Table 11, the consistency ratio is provided. The consistency ratio of 0.01 shows that the pair-wise comparison does not exceed 0.10 and is considered acceptable. The results of the information technology analyst survey and the AHP consistency index table (Table 11) show that firewalls are significantly (7.88) more effective at stopping DoS attacks, in comparison to the other four information assurance measures.

Table 9

Consistency Index	Effectiveness - Stopping Viruses						
	Firewalls	Antivirus	IDS	Passwords	Smartcards	Sum	W-Vector (Weight)
A. Firewalls (4.12)	0.35	0.27	0.27	0.27	0.27	1.44	7.22
B. Antivirus (3.89)	0.33	0.26	0.26	0.26	0.26	1.36	6.82
C. IDS (3.10)	0.26	0.21	0.21	0.21	0.21	1.09	5.43
D. Passwords (2.27)	0.19	0.15	0.15	0.15	0.15	0.80	3.98
E. Smartcards (1.63)	0.14	0.11	0.11	0.11	0.11	0.57	2.86
						Lambda	5.26
					Consistency Index	CI	0.05
					Consistency Ratio	CR	0.01

Effectiveness in Stopping Viruses Consistency Index

Note. p = cr < 0.10.

Table 10
Effectiveness in Stopping Hacking Consistency Index

Consistency Index	Effectiveness - Stopping Hacking						
	Firewalls	IDS	Passwords	Smartcards	Antivirus	Sum	W-Vector (Weight)
A. Firewalls (4.18)	0.35	0.28	0.28	0.28	0.28	1.46	7.32
B. IDS (3.69)	0.31	0.25	0.25	0.25	0.25	1.29	6.46
C. Passwords (2.80)	0.24	0.19	0.19	0.19	0.19	0.98	4.90
D. Smartcards (2.44)	0.21	0.16	0.16	0.16	0.16	0.85	4.27
E. Antivirus (1.93)	0.16	0.13	0.13	0.13	0.13	0.68	3.38
						Lambda	5.27
					Consistency Index	CI	0.05
					Consistency Ratio	CR	0.01

Note. p = cr < 0.10.

Table 11

Effectiveness in Stopping DoS Attacks Consistency Index

Consistency Index	Effectiveness - Stopping DOS Attack						
	Firewalls	IDS	Antivirus	Password	Smartcards	Sum	W-Vector (Weight)
A. Firewalls (4.46)	0.39	0.30	0.30	0.30	0.30	1.58	7.88
B. IDS (3.99)	0.35	0.27	0.27	0.27	0.27	1.41	7.05
C. Antivirus (2.33)	0.20	0.16	0.16	0.16	0.16	0.82	4.12
D. Passwords (2.12)	0.18	0.14	0.14	0.14	0.14	0.75	3.75
E. Smartcards (2.09)	0.18	0.14	0.14	0.14	0.14	0.74	3.69
						Lambda	5.30
					Consistency Index	CI	0.05
					Consistency Ratio	CR	0.01

Note. p = cr < 0.10.

Research Question

What is the relationship between an information technology analysts' prioritization of defense in-depth measures and the effectiveness in protecting organizational technology? The research question explores whether the analytical hierarchy process (AHP) can be used in the prioritization of information assurance defense in-depth measures to improve organizational information security.

Hypothesis

H_0 Null Hypothesis. AHP does not affect the relationship between the information technology analysts' prioritization of five defense in-depth dependent variables (anti-virus; firewalls; intrusion detection systems; passwords; and encryptions) and the independent variables of cost, ease of use, and effectiveness in protecting organizational devices against cyber-attacks.

H_1. AHP does affect the relationship between the information technology analysts' prioritization of five defense in-depth information assurance measures-the dependent variables–(anti-virus; firewalls; intrusion detection systems; passwords; and smartcards) and the independent variables of standard cost, perceived ease of use, and effectiveness in protecting organizational devices against cyber-attacks.

Based on the analysis of the consistency index (0.05) and consistency ratio (0.01) results, hypothesis H_0 for the research question is rejected; AHP does affect the relationship between the information technology analyst prioritization of five defense in-depth information assurance measures–the dependent variables–(anti-virus; firewalls; intrusion detection systems; passwords; and smartcards) and the independent variables of standard cost, perceived ease of use and effectiveness in protecting organizational devices against cyber-attacks.

Data Analysis and Results Summary

The research question for this study rejected the hypotheses H_0 which indicated that the data collected by the participants in the study show that AHP does affect the relationship between the information technology analysts prioritization of five defense in-depth information assurance measures–the dependent variables–(anti-virus; firewalls; intrusion detection systems; passwords; and smartcards) and the independent variables of standard cost, perceived ease of use, and effectiveness in protecting organizational devices against cyber-attacks. The implication of accepting the alternate H_0 Null Hypothesis, that AHP does not affect the relationship between the information technologies analysts' prioritization would mean that AHP is not an effective process in determining the prioritization of defense in-depth measures. The conclusions and recommendations for the study analyses results, as well as a model for furthering the field and application of frameworks and regulations are presented and discussed in the next chapter.

CHAPTER 5. DISCUSSION, IMPLICATIONS, RECOMMENDATIONS

Introduction

This chapter includes conclusions and recommendations made based on both the research and investigative questions. It also contains recommendations for further research on the use of AHP in the defense in-depth process, as well as additional continued related research. Finally, this chapter offers practical ways that AHP can be applied in the defense in-depth planning process.

Summary of the Results

Research Question

The research question explored whether the analytical hierarchy process (AHP) can be used in the prioritization of information assurance defense in-depth measures to improve organizational information security. What is the relationship between an information technology analyst's prioritization of defense in-depth measures and the effectiveness in protecting organizational devices?

Hypothesis

Hypothesis H_1. The AHP does affect the relationship between the information technology analysts' prioritization of five defense in-depth information assurance measures (dependent variables); anti-virus; firewalls; intrusion detection systems; passwords; and smartcards and the independent variables of standard cost, perceived ease of use, and effectiveness in protecting organizational devices against cyber-attacks. The first conclusion statistically proved that the AHP does affect the relationship between the information technology analyst prioritization of five defense in-depth information assurance measures and the standard cost, perceived ease of use, and effectiveness in protecting organizational devices against cyber-attacks.

Discussion of the Results

In addition to the main conclusions, the investigative questions findings also add to the knowledge of the subject. The conclusion using these findings of AHP prioritization consistency from the participants' survey responses provided cross-validation. The findings also added validity to the survey and study.

Investigative Question 1

Investigative Question 1 was of the five most common information assurance measures (anti-virus; firewalls; intrusion detection systems; passwords; and smartcards); rank them in terms of cost of implementation: 1 = *least costly* and 5 = *most costly*. The consistency ratio of 0.01 shows that the pair-wise comparison did not exceed 0.10, and is considered acceptable. Results from Investigative Question 1 indicated that through the ranking of the five defense in-depth measures by 100 U.S. information technology analysts and the results of the AHP, the measures can be ranked (1-5) in terms of their implementation cost in protecting organizational computing devices. The results show that passwords have moderately (6.55) less implementation cost than the other four information assurance measures. This knowledge could help in future considerations for reducing the cost of information assurance defense in-depth measures and in the evolution of the existing frameworks. The analytical prioritization, in this case of passwords, in comparison to other defense in-depth measures, could assist IT security personnel to adequately respond to the recurrent problems and contemporary challenges of cyber-attacks.

Investigative Question 2

Investigative Question 2 was of the five most common information assurance measures (firewalls, intrusion detection systems, anti-virus, passwords and smartcards); rank them in terms of maintenance cost: 1 = *least costly* and 5 = *most costly*. The consistency ratio of 0.01 shows that the pair-wise comparison did not exceed 0.10, and is considered acceptable. Results from Investigative Question 2 indicated that through the ranking of the 5 defense in-depth measures by 100 U.S. information technology analysts and the results of AHP, the measures can be ranked (1-5) in terms of their maintenance cost in protecting organizational computing devices. This knowledge could help in future considerations for reducing the maintenance cost of information assurance defense in-depth measures and in the evolution of the existing frameworks. The results of prioritizing defense in-depth measures in terms of maintenance costs could assist IT security personnel in reducing the problem of the inadequate and ineffective use of scientific principles, knowledge, and methods in the IA process.

Investigative Question 3

Investigative Question 3 asked, of the five most common information assurance measures (firewalls; intrusion detection systems; anti-virus; passwords; and smartcards); rank them in terms of Life-cycle Cost: 1 = *least costly* and 5 = *most costly*. The consistency ratio of 0.01 shows that the pair-wise comparison did not exceed 0.10, and is considered acceptable. Results from Investigative Question 3 indicate that through the ranking of the five defense in-depth measures by 100 U.S. Information technology analysts and the results of the AHP, the measures can be ranked (1-5) in terms of their life-cycle cost in protecting organizational computing devices. The results show that passwords have moderately (6.36) less life-cycle cost than the other four information   assurance measures. This knowledge could help in future considerations for reducing the life cycle cost of information assurance defense in-depth measures. By using AHP to prioritize the life-cycle cost of their defense in-depth measures, organizations could reduce the overall life-cycle cost of protecting their computing devices from the increasing problem of global computer criminalization.

Investigative Question 4

Investigative Question 4 was of the five most common information assurance measures (firewalls; intrusion detection systems; anti-virus; passwords; and smartcards); rank them in terms of the employees' ease of use: 1 = *easiest* and 5 = *most difficult*. The consistency ratio of 0.01 shows that the pair-wise comparison did not exceed the level of 0.10, and is considered acceptable. Results from Investigative Question 4 indicated that through the ranking of the 5 defense in-depth measures by 100 U.S. information technology analysts and the results of the AHP, the measures can be ranked (1-5) in terms of the employees' ease of use for in protecting organizational computing devices. This knowledge could help in the future to make considerations for information assurance defense in-depth measures easier for employees to use and in the evolution of the existing frameworks. The use of AHP to rank defense in-depth measures by ease of use could assist information technology analysts in the United States in solving the problem of effectively deploying information assurance defense in-depth measures to protect organizational computing devices within their organizations.

Investigative Question 5

Investigative Question 5 asked Of the five most common information assurance measures (firewalls; intrusion detection systems; anti-virus; passwords; and smartcards), rank them in terms of the technicians' ease of use for: 1 = *easiest to use* and 5 = *most difficult*. The consistency ratio of 0.01 shows that the pair-wise comparison did not exceed 0.10, and is considered acceptable. Results from Investigative Question 5 indicated that through the ranking of the five defense in-depth measures by 100 U.S. information technology analysts and the results of the AHP the measures can be ranked (1-5) in terms of the technicians' ease of use in protecting organizational computing devices.

The results showed that passwords were moderately (6.79) easier to use for technicians to use in comparison to the other four information assurance measures. This knowledge could help in future considerations for making information assurance defense in-depth measures easier for technicians to use and in the evolution of the existing frameworks. Using AHP to prioritize defense in-depth measures to make passwords easier for technicians to use could help solve the recurrent problems and contemporary challenges of cyber-attacks that conventional information assurance (IA) process guidance and practice fail to provide.

Investigative Question 6

Investigative Question 6 was of the five most common information assurance measures (firewalls; intrusion detection systems; anti-virus; passwords; and smartcards), rank them in terms of ease of use for management: 1 = *easiest to use* and 5 = *most difficult.* The consistency ratio of 0.01 showed that the pair-wise comparison did not exceed 0.10 and was considered acceptable.

Results from Investigative Question 6 indicated that through the ranking of the 5 defense in-depth measures by 100 U.S. information technology analysts and the results of the AHP, the measures can be ranked (1-5) in terms of the management's ease of use in protecting organizational computing devices. This knowledge could help in future considerations for making information assurance defense in-depth measures easier to manage and in the evolution of the existing frameworks. A network security approach which addresses security problems faced by national security organizations could be developed by using defense in-depth that were prioritized by AHP to make them easier for managers to use.

Investigative Question 7

Investigative Question 7 asked of the five most common information assurance measures (firewalls; intrusion detection systems; anti-virus; passwords; and smartcards); rank them in terms of effectively stopping viruses: 1 = *most effective* and 5 = *least effective.* The consistency ratio of 0.01 shows that the pair-wise comparison did not exceed 0.10, and is considered acceptable. Results from Investigative Question 7 indicated that through the ranking of the five defense in-depth measures by 100 U.S. information technology analysts and the results of the AHP, the measures can be ranked (1-5) in terms of their effectiveness in stopping viruses in the protection of organizational computing devices.

The results indicated that firewalls were significantly (7.22) more effective at preventing viruses in comparison to the other four information assurance measures. This knowledge could help in future considerations for selecting the prioritization of defense in-depth measures against viruses and in the evolution of the existing frameworks. The AHP prioritization of anti-virus defense in-depth techniques could be used to respond to the problem of network security against viruses and provide new knowledge by which to better deal with the problem.

Investigative Question 8

Investigative Question 8 was of the five most common information assurance measures (firewalls; intrusion detection systems; anti-virus; passwords; and smartcards); rank them in terms of effectiveness in stopping hacking: 1 = *most effective* and 5 = *least effective.* The consistency ratio of 0.01 shows that the pair-wise comparison did not exceed 0.10, and is considered acceptable. Results from Investigative Question 8 indicated that through the ranking of the 5 defense in-depth measures by 100 U.S. information technology analysts and the results of the AHP, the measures can be ranked (1-5) in terms of their effectiveness in stopping hacking in the protection of organizational computing devices. The results showed that firewalls are significantly (7.32) more effective at reducing hacking attacks in comparison to the other four information assurance measures. This knowledge could help in future considerations for choosing information assurance defense in-depth measures to prevent hacking attacks and in the evolution of the existing frameworks. AHP could be used to prioritize defense in-depth measures against hackers to prevent persistent attacks that present a problem for network defenses.

Investigative Question 9

Investigative Question 9 asked, of the five most common information assurance measures (firewalls; intrusion detection systems; anti-virus; passwords; and smartcards); rank them in terms of effectiveness in stopping denial of service attacks: 1 = *most effective* and 5 = *least effective*. The consistency ratio of 0.01 shows that the pair-wise comparison did not exceed 0.10, and is considered acceptable. Results from Investigative Question 9 indicated that through the ranking of the five defense in-depth measures by 100 U.S. information technology analysts and the results of the Analytical Hierarchy Process (AHP), the measures can be ranked (1-5) in terms of their effectiveness in stopping denial of service attacks against organizational computing devices. The AHP pair-wise comparison of denial of service attack measures could be used by companies to solve cybersecurity-related events that have become an increasing problem for organizations, such as the oil and gas industry over the past decade.

Implications

The knowledge gained from this investigation can help in the prioritization of information assurance defense in-depth and in the evolution of the existing frameworks. The results show that passwords are moderately (6.26) easier for management to use in comparison to the other four information assurance measures and can be used by managers who have less information assurance training. Passwords also have moderately (6.38) less maintenance cost than the other four information assurance measures and can be used by organizations that operate on a limited budget. Additionally, firewalls are slightly (5.70) easier for employees to use in comparison to the other four information assurance measures. This can make it easier for personnel intensive organizations to prioritize defense in-depth measures. The results show that firewalls are significantly (7.88) more effective at stopping DoS attacks in comparison to the other four information assurance measures can be used to lower the number of attacks that organizations face.

Limitations

A limitation of this study is that only registered Survey Monkey members with the title of information technology analyst were contacted for their opinions on the defense in-depth measures. This non-experimental survey research design was used to survey a simple random sample of 954 active Survey Monkey registered information

technology analysts from a population of 78,020. Although there may be minor differences in the opinions of information technology analysts, results can be statically generalizable to the entire population of information technology analysts in the United States.

The lack of prioritization of the lines of defense is a limitation of this research, although Hoff's information helped to establish the study's relevance and significance within the field of defense in-depth. Inadequate security strategies, as outlined by Mazu Networks (2005), characterized the recommendations and implications for future research as justification for this study. Mazu Networks (2005) delved into the complicated challenges presented by today's ever-evolving network and discusses why current security strategies inadequately protect critical internal assets. The non-experimental research design and theoretical framework of this study addressed the lack of adequate security discussed in the Mazu Networks (2005) information.

Additional Related Research Recommendations

The illustrations in Tables 1 through 9 depict the different rankings of the information assurance defense in-depth measures. Contrasts in the rankings of the data collected indicated significant differences in the measures based on the three summarized multiple-response variables: standard cost, perceived effectiveness, and ease of use. The study did not explore this contrast. Given the significance of this data, this area would represent an important area for further exploratory study.

Recommendations for Further Research

Recommendations for future research based on this research study's results include the following:

1.   Specific measurements and analyses of information assurance defense in-depth procedures provide additional data to defense in-depth decision makers when prioritizing defense in-depth measures.

2.   Specific measurements and analyses of information assurance procedures used in organizations may give defense in-depth decision makers greater insight into how well their organizations are protected.

3. Specific measurements and analyses of this study's developed IT security effectiveness construct may allow defense in-depth decision makers to uses AHP in creative ways to enhance organizational IT security.

The research concluded that the AHP process can play a role in the IT security of organizations. Further research of the current use of defense in-depth and potential weaknesses of current information assurance procedures may help advance IT security overall.

The research conclusion that the AHP process can be used to prioritize defense in-depth measures is affirmed, given the significant amount of AHP knowledge that is published. The integration of the AHP process in defense in-depth decision-making can help to improve IT security. The use and implementation of AHP to prioritize defense in-depth measures could be an added asset in many organizations.

Future research into the AHP, especially related to IT security may help improve the understanding of how to design and deploy defense in-depth measures. This study also proposed an AHP structural and measurement model to help determine important factors in better understanding and implementing AHP in IT security solutions. The future of IT security should include additional exploratory models to advance understanding of why the current models are not substantially improving IT security.

REFERENCES

Alexander, M. (2012*). Making use of the analytic hierarchy process (AHP) and SAS/IML.* Baltimore, MD: Social Security Administration.

Al-Harbi, K. (2001). Application of the AHP in project management. *International Journal of Project Management, 19*(1), 19-27. doi:10.1016/s0263-7863 (99)00038-1

Andrews, D., Nonnecke, B., & Preece, J. (2003). Electronic survey methodology: A case study in reaching hard-to-involve Internet users. *International Journal of Human–Computer Interaction, 16*(2), 185–210. doi:10.1207/s15327590ijhc1602_04

Armstrong, P. (n.d.) Bloom's taxonomy. Retrieved from https://cft.vanderbilt.edu/guides-sub-pages/blooms-taxonomy/

Australian Communications and Media Authority. (2015). [Home page]. Retrieved from http://www.acma.gov.au.

Bakolas, E., & Saleh, J. (2011). Augmenting defense-in-depth with the concepts of observability and diagnosability from control theory and discrete event systems. *Reliability Engineering & System Safety, 96*(1), 184-193. doi:10.1016/j.ress.2010. 09.002

Barnes, N. D., & Barnes, F. (2012). Smartphone technologies shine spotlight on information governance. *Information Management Journal, 46*(3), 40-43. Retrieved from http://content.arma.org/IMM/Libraries/May-June_2012/ IMM_0512_Tech_Trends_Smartphone_Technologies.sflb.ashx

Basagiannis, S., Petridou, S., Alexiou, N., Papadimitriou, G., & Katsaros, P. (2011). Quantitative analysis of a certified e-mail protocol in mobile environments: A probabilistic model checking approach. *Computers & Security, 30*(4), 257-272. doi:10.1016/j.cose.2011.02.001

Biesecker, C. (2010). DHS IG finds adequate cybersecurity controls but more needed. *Defense Daily, 247*(49), 8.

Blitz, T. (2005). Decoding mobile device security. *Security, 42*(5), 46.

Bond, I. (2004, October 6). Defense in-depth. *Computer Weekly*, 43.

Brooke, P. (2001). Building an in-depth defense. *Network Computing, 12*(14), 75-77.

Bryant, M. T. (2005). Managing an effective and ethical research project. In R. A. Swanson & E. F. Holton, III (Eds.), *Research in organizations: Foundations and methods of inquiry* (pp. 419–436). San Francisco, CA: Berrett-Koehler.

Bureau of Labor Statistics, U.S. Department of Labor. (2015). *Labor force statistics from the current population survey.* Retrieved from http://www.bls.gov/cps/cpsaat 11.htm

Byres, E. (2014). Defense-in-depth: Reliable security to thwart cyber-attacks. *Pipeline & Gas Journal, 241*(2), 58-60. Retrieved from https://pgjonline.com/ 2014/02/12/defense-in-depth-reliable-security-to-thwart-cyber-attacks/

Cheng, E. W. L., Li, H., & Ho, D. C. K. (2002). Analytic hierarchy process (AHP). *Measuring Business Excellence, 6*(4), 33-37. doi:10.1108/13683040210451697

Cleghorn, L. (2013). Network defense methodology: A comparison of defense in-depth and defense in breadth. *Journal of Information Security, 4*(3), 144-149. doi: 10.4236/jis.2013.43017

Cobb, M. (2014, November). Firewall. Retrieved from http://searchsecurity.techtarget. com/definition/firewall

Cobb, M., & Meckley, J. (2016, October). Smart card. Retrieved from http://search
    security.techtarget.com/definition/smart-card

Cole, B. (2014, June). Intrusion detection system. Retrieved from http://search
    compliance.techtarget.com/definition/intrusion-detection-systems-IDS

Cooper, C. R., & Schindler, P. S. (2008). *Business research methods* (10th ed.). Boston, MA: McGraw-Hill.

Creswell, J. W. (2009). *Research design: Qualitative, quantitative, and mixed methods approaches* (3rd ed.). Los Angeles,
    CA: Sage.

Davis, F. D. (1989). Perceived usefulness, perceived ease of use, and user acceptance of information technology. *MIS
    Quarterly, 13*(3), 319-340. doi:10.2307/249008

de Reuver, M., Bouwman, H., Prieto, G., & Visser, A. (2011). Governance of flexible mobile service platforms. *Futures,
    43*(9), 979-985. doi:10.1016/j.futures.2011.
    06.007

Effectiveness. BusinessDictionary.com. Retrieved January 17, 2017, from BusinessDictionary.com website:
    http://www.businessdictionary.com/definition/effectiveness.html

Fan, X. (2010). *Data dissemination and sharing in mobile computing environments* (Doctotal dissertation).Retrieved from
    ProQuest Dissertations & Theses Global. (Order No. 3448498)

Faul, F., Erdfelder, E., Buchner, A., & Lang, A. (2009). Statistical power analyses using GPower 3.1: Tests for correlation
    and regression analyses. *Behavior Research Methods, 41*(4), 1,149-1,160. doi:10.3758/BRM.41.4.1149

Fofana, M. I. (2010). *E-government technical security controls taxonomy for information assurance contractors---a
    relational approach* (Doctoral dissertation). ProQuest Dissertations & Theses Global. (855603420)

Gandhi, R., Sharma, A., Mahoney, W., Sousan, W., Qiuming, Z., & Laplante, P. (2011). Dimensions of cyber-attacks:
    Cultural, social, economic, and political. *Technology and Society Magazine, IEEE, 30*(1), 28-38.
    doi:10.1109/MTS.
    2011.940293

Geoff, C. (2004). *The analytic hierarchy process (AHP).* Upper Saddle River, NJ: Pearson Education.

Harris, J. (2005, September). Antivirus software. Retrieved from http://searchsecurity.
    techtarget.com/definition/antivirus-software

Hinkin, T. R. (2005). Scale development principles and practices. In R. A. Swanson & E. F. Holton, III (Eds.), *Research in
    organizations: Foundations and methods of inquiry* (pp. 161–179). San Francisco, CA: Berrett-Koehler.

Hirschmann, J. (2014). Defense in-depth: A layered approach to network security. *Security, 51*(9), 95. Retrieved from
    http://www.securitymagazine.com/articles/
    85788-defense-in-depth-a-layered-approach-to-network-security

Hoff, B. (2004). Storage infrastructure requires defense in-depth. *Computer Technology Review, 24*(7), 32-33.

Holton, E. F., III., & Burnett, M. F. (2005). The basics of quantitative research. In R. A. Swanson & E. F. Holton, III
    (Eds.), *Research in organizations: Foundations and methods of inquiry* (pp. 11–26). San Francisco, CA: Berrett-
    Koehler.

Huntley, V. (2010). Data security in a real-time world requires "defense in-depth" strategy. *National Underwriter P & C,
    114*(25), 18-19.

Jackson, W. (2004, February 4). ONI counts on defense-in-depth, redundancy for its nets. Retrieved from Government Computer News: http://www.lexisnexis.com/hottopics/lnacademic.

Johna, T. J. (2004). Security today means playing "defense-in-depth." *Network World, 21*(33), 24. Retrieved from http://www.networkworld.com/article/2324961/lan-wan/security-today-means-playing--defense-in-depth-.html

Lavrakas, P. J. (Ed.). (2008). *Encyclopedia of survey research methods.* Thousand Oaks, CA: Sage.

Lawrence, D. P. (2013). *Impact assessment: Practical solutions to recurrent problems and contemporary* (2nd ed.). Hoboken, NJ: Wiley & Sons.

Liu, S. (2010). Supporting a mobile workforce. *IT Professional Magazine, 12*(3), 4-5. doi:10.1109/MITP.2010.96

Luallen, M., & Hamburg, S. (2009). Applying security defense-in-depth. *Control Engineering, 56*(12), 49-51. Retrieved from http://www.controleng.com/

Mazu Networks, Inc. (2005, November 7). Enterprise strategy group publishes research identifying network behavior analysis systems as the new foundation of defense-in-depth (Press release). Retrieved from PR Newswire Association: http://www.prnewswire.com/news-releases/enterprise-strategy-group-publishes-research-identifying-network-behavior-analysis-systems-as-the-new-foundation-of-defense-in-depth-55415267.html

Moon, D., Im, H., Lee, J. D., & Park, J. H. (2014). MLDS: Multi-layer defense system for preventing advanced persistent threats. *Symmetry, 6*(4), 997-1,010. doi:10.3390/sym6040997

Passmore, D. L., & Baker, R. M. (2005). Sampling strategies and power analysis. In R. A. Swanson & E. F. Holton, III (Eds.), *Research in organizations: Foundations and methods of inquiry* (pp. 221–232). San Francisco, CA: Berrett-Koehler.

Rouse, M. (2007a, June). Defense in depth. Retrieved from http://searchsecurity.techtarget.com/definition/defense-in-depth

Rouse, M. (2007b, June). Password. Retrieved from http://searchsecurity.techtarget.com/definition/password

Saaty, T. L. (1994). How to make a decision: The analytic hierarchy process. *Interfaces, 24*(6), 19-43. doi:10.1287/inte.24.6.19

Sedzro, K., Marouane, A., & Assogbavi, T. (2012). Analytical hierarchy process and goal programming approach for asset allocation. *Journal of Mathematical Finance, 2*(1), 96-104. doi:10.4236/jmf.2012.21012

Shehab, M., & Marouf, S. (2012), Recommendation models for open authorization. *IEEE Transactions on Dependable and Secure Computing, 9*(4), 583-596. doi: 10.1109/tdsc.2012.34

Standard cost. (n.d.). In *Business Dictionary*: http://www.businessdictionary.com/definition/standard-cost.html

Stephenson, P. (2012). Endpoint security. *SC Magazine, 23*(8), 32. Retrieved from https://www.scmagazine.com/eset-endpoint-security/review/6640/

Straub, D., Boudreau, M.-C., & Gefen, D. (2004). Validation guidelines for IS positivist research. *Communications of the Association for Information Systems, 13,* 380–427. Retrieved from http://aisel.aisnet.org/cais/vol13/iss1/24

Uncertainty abounds. (2012). *Computer Reseller News, 17*. Retrieved from http://www.channelweb.co.uk/crn-uk/analysis/2179491/uncertainty-abounds

U.S. Department of Health & Human Services. (1979, April 18). *The Belmont report*. Retrieved from http://www.hhs.gov/ohrp/humansubjects/guidance/belmont.html

Utugizaki, M., Udagawa, M., Shinohara, M., & Osawa, K. (2007). Consistency index for the whole decision making. In *Proceedings of DEA Symposium 2007* (pp. 102-105). Osaka, Japan: Osaka University.

Vaidya, O., & Kumar, S. (2006). Analytic hierarchy process: An overview of applications. *European Journal of Operational Research, 169*(1), 1-29. doi:10.1016/j.ejor.2004.04.028

Viega, J., & Michael, B. (2010). Guest editors' introduction: Mobile device security. *IEEE Security & Privacy Magazine, 8*(2), 11-12. doi: 10.1109/MSP.2010.76

Vogt, W. P. (2007). *Quantitative research methods for professionals*. Boston, MA: Pearson Custom.

Warner, C. (2013). Wireless networks balance military's defense-in-depth, custom requirements. *ECN: Electronic Component News, 57*(5), 12-14. Retrieved from https://www.ecnmag.com/article/2013/05/wireless-networks-balance-militarys-defense-depth-custom-requirements

Wind, Y., & Saaty, T. L. (1980). Marketing applications of the analytic hierarchy process. *Management Science, 26*(7), 641-658. doi:10.1287/mnsc.26.7.641

Yang, B. (2005). Factor analysis methods. In R. A. Swanson & E. F. Holton, III (Eds.), *Research in organizations: Foundations and methods of inquiry* (pp. 181-199). San Francisco, CA: Berrett-Koehler.

APPENDIX A. DATA COLLECTION INSTRUMENT

A simple random sample of 100 Survey-Monkey.com registered information technology analysts from a population of 78,020 information technology analysts in the United States were e-mailed a survey, asking them to prioritize from 1 to 5, five defense in-depth measures based on cost, ease of use, and prevention ability.

1. Of the five most common information assurance measures (firewalls, intrusion detection systems, passwords and smartcards), rank them in terms of cost of implementing: 1 = *least costly* and 5 = *most costly.*

2. Of the five most common information assurance measures (firewalls, intrusion detection systems, anti-virus, passwords and smartcards), rank them in terms of maintenance cost: 1 = *least costly* and 5 = *most costly.*

3. Of the five most common information assurance measures (firewalls, intrusion detection systems, anti-virus, passwords and smartcards), rank them in terms of life-cycle cost: 1 = *least costly* and 5 = *most costly.*

4. Of the five most common information assurance measures (firewalls, intrusion detection systems, anti-virus, passwords and smartcards), rank them in terms of ease of use for employees: 1 = *easiest* and 5 = *most difficult.*

5. Of the five most common information assurance measures (firewalls, intrusion detection systems, passwords and smartcards), rank them in terms of ease of use for technicians: 1 = *easiest to use* and 5 = *most difficult.*

6. Of the five most common information assurance measures (firewalls, intrusion detection systems, passwords and smartcards), rank them in terms of effectively stopping viruses: 1 = *most effective* and 5 = *least effective.*

7. Of the five most common information assurance measures (firewalls, intrusion detection systems, anti-virus, passwords and smartcards), rank them in terms of effectiveness in stopping hacking: 1 = *most effective* and 5 = *least effective.*

8. Of the five most common information assurance measures (firewalls, intrusion detection systems, passwords and smartcards), rank them in terms of ease of use for management: 1 = *easiest to use* and 5 = *most difficult.*

9. Of the five most common information assurance measures (firewalls, intrusion detection systems, anti-virus, passwords and smartcards), rank them in terms of effectiveness in stopping hacking: 1 = *most effective* and 5 = *least effective.*

10. Administrative Question: Informed Consent Request.

www.ingramcontent.com/pod-product-compliance
Lightning Source LLC
Chambersburg PA
CBHW082111070326
40689CB00052B/4574